25 Years in India
A Personal Story of Upheaval, Culture Shock, Survival, and Transformation

Elma E. Vaidya

Enjoy Reading
Elma Vaidya

Copyright © 2016 by Elma E. Vaidya.

All rights reserved. No part of this book may be reproduced in any form or by any electronic or mechanical means including information storage and retrieval systems, without permission in writing from the author. The only exception is by a reviewer, who may quote short excerpts in a review.

Design by J. Putnam Design www.jputnamdesign.com

ISBN-13: 978-1-523-42328-6
ISBN-10: 1-523-42328-5

For my loving husband, Madhu Vaidya

Contents

Acknowledgments vii
Preface ix
Part I: Getting Started 1
   1. Uprooted 2
   2. Beginnings 15
   3. Shimla: A Long Wait for a Job 21
   4. Tough Times 25
   5. Babu-ji 29
   6. Special Delivery at Snowdon Hospital 34
   7. Job Celebration 41
   8. Move to Rohru 46
   9. Bumpy Bus Ride in the Mountains 50
  10. Following the Rivers and Setting up a Home 56
  11. Fishing in Himachal Pradesh 62
  12. A Trip to Mandi and a Forest Inspection Tour 66
  13. Ice Skating at Shimla 69
  14. The Unexpected 73

Part II: Carrying On 77
  15. Landslides in the Dodra Kwar Area 78
  16. American and Indian Deliveries 89
  17. Wait—Wait—Wait 94
  18. My First Teaching Job in India 98

Part III: Visits from American Family 103
  19. Mother's First Impressions of Delhi 104
  20. Visit to Jaipur 107
  21. Delhi to Chamba via Pathankot 111
  22. Mother's Stay at Chamba 117
  23. Family Visit from Pennsylvania 122

Part IV: Amalgamation 137
  24. Surprising Comments by Friends 138
  25. Nomination or Not 140
  26. My Own Return to College 145
  27. Ama-ji 150

Part V: Coming Home 154
  28. Return to America 155

29. United States to Kulu	157
30. Stay at Mandi	160
31. Jogindernagar Visit	166
32. Day Trip to Dharamsala Area	172
33. Raj Kumar's Mandi Visit	177
35. Sharing the Draft of My Memoir with Indian Family and Friends	181

Epilogue	185
Appendices	187
Appendix A: Bucket in a Well	188
Appendix B: A Letter from Madhu	190
Appendix C: Before and Now: India in the 1960s and India in the 21st Century	192
Glossary	199

Acknowledgments

The initial credit for this memoir goes to my mother, Louise Griscom. In 1965, while I was visiting my parents in Michigan, she insisted that I take a writing course. In that class, I started my memoir. Throughout the years that followed, she continued to encourage me to write. During her two visits to India, she kept journals, which I later used to describe her stay.

My Aunt Elma also visited me in India. As I worked on this book, I was able to use the information in her travel journal and the brochures that she collected during her stay.

My husband, Madhu Vaidya, was the main reason for this memoir. Our relationship changed my life in an unexpected direction. After our marriage and move to India, he stood by me as I struggled to adjust.

Others who deserve credit are my father-in-law, Tej Singh Vaidya, and my mother-in-law, Sarla Devi Vaidya. They welcomed and accepted their American daughter-in-law, who was different from anyone they ever knew.

My children, Tara and Rita, helped me in piecing together my stories. My sons-in-law, (Richard Ricardi and John Eskew), offered suggestions for revisions. Grandsons, (Caleb, Ethan, Nathaniel, Krishan, and Vishnu), read parts and made helpful comments.

The facilitators and class members in the three writing classes I took over the years were frank and helpful with their critiquing. I am grateful for the support of my teachers and peers at the Birmingham Community House in 1965, my professional development writing class at the Rogers Middle School in the 1990s, and my current shared writing group at Rivier Institute for Senior Education in Nashua, New Hampshire.

My editor Renée M. Nicholls was a huge help with her many beneficial suggestions. Thanks also to Jenny Putnam for her design work.

Preface

Wearing a knee-length, white wedding dress on a bitter cold day at the start of 1962, I was married in a suburban Presbyterian Church to my fiancé, Madhu, who was nicknamed Steve.[1] Despite the Michigan snow and wind, American family and friends, along with a few Indian friends, came to celebrate the occasion. Six months later, wearing a maroon sari[2] embroidered with silver threads on a sweltering June day, I was married a second time to Madhu in a Delhi Arya Samaj[3] temple. All the guests were Indian, and I was visibly pregnant. During the ceremony, I didn't know what was happening. I couldn't understand the Sanskrit language spoken by the officiating *pandit* (scholarly religious leader).

This Arya Samaj ceremony was one of my early introductions to Indian customs. I was a young American woman who was about to be educated in the differences between India and the United States. Before my move to India, I'd had little experience with people of different races, religions, and ethnicity. The move to India was my first trip outside of the country except for short visits to Canada.

My Indian journey, which lasted from 1962 to the late 1980s, included speed bumps, detours, and smooth roads. Living in remote ar-

---

[1] Throughout the memoir, I shift back and forth from using Steve to *Madhu*, depending on who is talking about him and the situation. When I started dating Steve at Duke University, I knew him by his American nickname. His friends in Durham and my family all called him Steve. In India, he was known as Madhu, his birth name. After being in India for a few years, I started calling him Madhu, but reverted back to Steve when my American family came for visits.

[2] A sari consists of a drape anywhere from five to nine yards (4.57 metres to 8.23 metres) in length and two to four feet (60 cm to 1.20 m) in breadth that is wrapped around the waist, with one end draped over the shoulder. A short, fitted blouse that bares the midriff is worn with it.

[3] A sect of the Hindu religion which was founded by Swami Dayananda.

eas of Himachal Pradesh without the company of other Americans, I faced many challenges. I had to learn Hindi, adapt to new customs, develop a taste for Indian food, accept long waits, raise a family, take college exams, and become part of my Indian family. Over the years, I gradually made my way from suffocation and culture shock to survival and transformation. My memoir provides a rough map of my journey.

part 1
Getting Started

Uprooted

In June of 1962, I walked through the low doorway of the air-conditioned Air India Boeing 707 and was greeted with a blast of Delhi air. It felt like shifting from a freezer into an oven. I followed Steve down the steps of the ramp to the black asbestos runway. By the time I reached the ground, the wind had made a mess of my short brown hair. When I opened my large wicker handbag, I was relieved to find my comb on the top, but it did little good as the hot air continued blowing. *What would my in-laws think of their American daughter-in-law?* I wanted to make a good impression, and already I had a problem.

Steve put his hand on my arm and said, "You look fine. Just put a big smile on your face. Everyone will love you."

We followed the passengers toward the immigration and customs area. Behind the wire fence that was next to the building, I saw a large group of people waving at the arriving passengers. The women were dressed in brightly colored Indian clothes and stood out from the men, who were dressed in plain suits, slacks, and shirts like those that men wore to offices and to churches in the United States. Steve pointed out his mother in the crowd, and we both waved.

Before we could join his family, our passports and luggage had to be checked. We entered a bare room with a few overhead fans that did little to alleviate the oppressive heat. The immigration officer looked at my American passport and instructed me to register with the American Embassy and the local police department. Next, he checked Steve's

Indian passport, which took much longer. There were many entries, since Steve had extended his student visa several times during his six years at Duke University's School of Forestry. Steve turned the pages of his passport, showing that the extensions were up to date.

Finally, the uniformed official was satisfied. In English he said, "Welcome home. I hope your wife likes India."

His comment made me think of how well Steve had adjusted to American customs. I hoped I would adjust as well to life in India. For the last few months, I had been trying to learn about my new home by auditing a course in Hindi, writing a research paper about *satyagraha* (passive resistance or truth experiments, as Gandhi preferred), and spending time with our Indian graduate school friends. The women had taught me to cook Indian food, and the men had discussed politics and living conditions in India. I had listened carefully to their discussions, hoping to learn more about Steve's country.

Still, I was anxious about whether I would be accepted by my in-laws. The recent letters from my father-in-law had been warm and friendly, but I knew the family was disappointed about our marriage. Before Steve left India to study at Duke, his family had arranged his engagement with a woman who lived in his hometown of Mandi and was from the same caste. When he told his parents of our upcoming marriage, they had to inform the woman's family that the engagement was off. I'm sure it was extremely embarrassing. It was bad enough that their only son didn't marry this woman from his hometown, but to marry a foreigner of his own choice was in complete opposition to their traditions.

My worrying was interrupted by a customs inspector who asked us to open our suitcases and declare the contents. As I opened the second bag, a smiling bald man came into the customs area and greeted Steve: "*Namaste*, Madhu-ji." For the first time, I truly understood that I would be the only one in India using his American nickname.

Steve introduced me to this man as Rattan Uncle and said that he was a lawyer and lived in Delhi. Uncle spoke directly to me. "Hello! I'm related to Madhu's mother. How was your trip?" I was relieved to hear him speak in perfect English.

"The trip went well. Nice to meet you."

Then Uncle turned to the inspector. "These are my relatives; take good care of them."

Hearing this, the official quickly completed his inspection.

Arrival at Delhi International Airport

Steve, Rattan Uncle, and I walked into the arrival room, where the family was waiting. Steve gave my hand a squeeze of encouragement. The room was crowded with people, and as we entered, a large group of Indian men, women, and children surrounded us. I wondered who all these people were. Steve and I became separated. The last thing I heard him say was, "Don't forget to touch their feet." Everybody was talking at once, and the language sounded alien. I felt lost in the crowd of unfamiliar faces.

The Hindi I had learned in my college class didn't seem to help with the loud talking and strange accents. All I understood was "Namaste-ji" as family members greeted me. I replied, "Namaste-ji" and touched their feet. Indian tradition only required me to touch the feet of those my age or older, but I didn't try to decipher their ages and did it for all the adults. Some family members put garlands of flowers and rupees around my neck.

Steve returned, and I could hardly see his face covered by the many garlands of orange marigold flowers and necklaces of green rupees that he was now wearing. He tried to encourage me and said, "You're doing great."

I wasn't so sure. In fact, I felt a little dizzy with the stifling heat and so many people crowding around me. There must have been at least thirty of them. A part of me felt like a celebrity, but another part was overwhelmed. *Will I learn the language? Will my in-laws accept me? Will I like this new life?*

As Steve pushed the garlands away from his face, his special smile made me feel a little more comfortable. The crowd around us moved back. An older man stepped forward, with a woman slightly behind him. The man had graying hair and wore a dark-colored suit with a Nehru suit coat that buttoned up to his neck.

Steve said, "I want you to meet my father, *Babu-ji*."[4]

I touched his feet. He thanked me and spoke softly in English. "Welcome to India."

Then Steve introduced me to his mother, *Ama-ji*.[5] Her face was partially covered with a long chiffon *dupatta* (scarf) draped around her head and shoulders. The dupatta was pulled down over her forehead. Still, I noticed the *bindi* (red dot) on her forehead and the sparkling diamond on her nose. She wore a pistachio-green outfit called a *salwar kameez*, which included Indian-style baggy pants and a long shirt. Her jeweled sandals were also green. I touched her feet also. My mother-in-law spoke to me in Hindi, and Steve translated for us, saying that she was glad we had gotten here safely.

I said, "Thank you." I hoped my grasp of Hindi would strengthen, so we could talk without a translator.

Next, I met Steve's sisters. As a greeting, we each pressed our palms and fingers together as if praying and said, "Namaste-ji." I spoke to them in English, which Steve had told me they knew, but they replied in Hindi. Two of his sisters wore embroidered silk saris in pastel colors. The third sister wore a salwar kameez.

The sisters seemed bashful and kept the top of their heads covered. The youngest sister's sari slipped off her head, and I could see how beautiful she was. All of Steve's sisters had red dots on their foreheads and diamond studs on their noses. Two sisters put garlands of marigolds around my neck, and a third one gave me a bouquet of flowers.

A tall young man approached us, and Steve said, "This is Rajinder. We went to high school together."

Quietly, Steve told Rajinder that after living in the United States for

---

[4] Babu-ji's full name was Tej Singh Vaidya, but he was rarely called by name because of his age and senior position in the family.

[5] Ama-ji's full name was Sarla Devi Vaidya. Like Babu-ji, she was rarely called by name.

so long, he couldn't recognize some of his relatives and friends. I knew I'd never remember who all these people were. Everybody had black hair, and they seemed to have similar features. The women wore their hair in a bun or a single braid hanging down their back. The little girls wore dresses slightly longer than the current American fashion. The young boys wore shorts and white dress shirts. After the introductions were over, the only people I knew for certain were Babu-ji, Ama-ji, Rattan Uncle, and Rajinder. I recognized Steve's sisters, but not by name.

As we prepared to leave the Delhi International Airport, which lacked modern amenities and looked like a domestic, small-town airport, Rajinder suggested that we go to a restaurant. Most of the family hadn't eaten breakfast, and it would be easier to get acquainted there. Our group of at least thirty relatives and friends headed for the parking lot, where we divided into smaller groups for the ride into central Delhi. Babu-ji, Ama-ji, Steve, one of his sisters, and I got into a black taxi with a bearded, turbaned Sikh driver. Throughout the ride, the family talked in Hindi. Occasionally Steve's father translated the conversations for me, but it was difficult for him to keep up. Often, several people talked at the same time. Steve hadn't seen his family for six years, and everyone asked many questions.

Three-wheelers in Delhi traffic

Our taxi was the first to reach the restaurant. I got out and was immediately surrounded by dirty, half-clothed children holding out small cups with a few coins and rupees in them. I felt sorry for these beggars and wanted to give them money. However, Rajinder warned me, "Don't give them anything. Once you start, they'll never stop pestering you."

Steve steered me towards an impressive-looking restaurant with a big sign on the front window that said "Air Conditioned." As we walked towards the entrance, I was surprised to see a cow lumbering across the busy street. All the vehicles stopped to let the cow cross safely.

Family members led the way into the restaurant. A strong smell of frying onions and spices greeted me, along with the host, who led us up a narrow, dark stairway. I entered the upstairs dining room and noticed that the furniture was shoddy and the air conditioner wasn't much help. A white-turbaned waiter guided us to a long banquet table in the center of the room. Another waiter came up to our table and cleared the crumbs off with a stained piece of cloth.

Rattan Uncle seated Steve's youngest sister next to me. He suggested that Steve walk around the room and meet people. Steve agreed and said, "Hansa will take care of you. She speaks English."

I wondered if she really did. I hadn't heard any English from his three sisters. I smiled at Hansa, and she smiled back. I remembered her beautiful face from the airport introduction. Neither of us spoke for a minute.

Then, with a slight Indian accent, Hansa asked, "What would you like for breakfast?"

I was surprised and said, "Oh! You do speak English!"

She replied, "Yes, but I was afraid you wouldn't understand me. I speak so poorly."

I assured her that she spoke English well. Then the waiter approached us, and Hansa spoke to him in Hindi. I was not feeling hungry. We had eaten breakfast on the plane, and watching the waiter use the same dirty cloth for cleaning everything had squelched my appetite considerably. I decided to try some Hindi and slowly said, *"Ek cup chai."* ("One cup of tea.")

The waiter spoke in English. "What did you say?"

I was disappointed that he didn't understand my Hindi, so I reluctantly resorted to English: "Please give me a cup of tea."

Hansa insisted that I have something to eat, so I asked for toast and tea. When the waiter brought them, I wished I had only ordered tea. The toast was served on a greasy plate. I drank the tea but ignored the toast. Everybody around me was talking loudly and enjoying their spicy-smelling breakfast of vegetable cutlets, potato and pea curry, *poori* (fried Indian bread), and many other Indian dishes.

After finishing breakfast and making a few more feeble attempts to speak Hindi, I felt tired. Steve inquired about where we would be staying. Along with Steve's three sisters, his father and mother, two brothers-in-law, two nephews, and a niece, none of whom lived in Delhi, we would be staying as guests at the home of a family friend who was vacationing in the mountains. Everyone else in the group from out of town was scattered around at the local homes of friends and relatives in nearby areas so we would be able to meet up and spend time together.

We all left the restaurant for our assigned homes. Rattan Uncle came in our taxi to give directions. When we arrived at the bungalow, he checked the taxi meter on the dashboard to make sure the driver didn't overcharge us. Uncle took his responsibilities seriously. He lived in Delhi so he knew how things operated, whereas other family members from Mandi weren't so familiar with Delhi.

When we went into the house, Steve's sister noticed how sleepy we looked. She led us to a sparsely furnished bedroom with a double bed and a small bedside table. Steve searched for the ceiling fan control and turned it on, but the fan only circulated hot air in the bedroom. The heat and the excitement of our arrival made me drowsy. I lay down on the bed and was surprised at how hard it was. I lifted the thin cotton mattress and saw it was lying on a piece of plywood.

At five o'clock in the evening, I woke up dripping wet with perspiration. I wanted to take a shower. Steve, who was also covered in perspiration, was still sleeping by my side. Quietly I got up and went into the living room, where I found everybody sprawled on the floor taking naps. My in-laws were not used to the hot weather. They lived in the mountains of Himachal Pradesh, where it was much cooler.

When Hansa heard me, she sat up and asked what I wanted. I said, "Where is the bathroom for taking a shower?"

She led me through an open courtyard at the back of the house and then into the shower room, which was separate from the rest of the house. I saw a waist-high faucet and an empty bucket but no shower or bathtub. I felt silly asking her how I was supposed to take a shower when there was no shower.

I decided to go back to the bedroom and ask Steve about the bathroom. He laughed when he heard my questions and walked me back to the shower room. He explained, "The small metal cup is called a *lotha*. Fill this bucket full of water. Sit on the small wooden stool, and dip the lotha into the water. Pour water from the lotha on yourself, soap yourself, and then pour more water to rinse off."

I tried my first Indian shower. The cool water felt refreshing, and I soaped myself generously to get rid of the perspiration and dust.

After my bucket shower, I felt hungry and went into the kitchen.

Steve's sister Anjana was boiling milk, and she gave me a glass of hot milk. It tasted strange, but I drank it, since I was pregnant and knew I should be increasing my intake of calcium. After finishing it, I asked Steve why it tasted and smelled so funny. He said, "It's buffalo milk, which has to be boiled several times to keep it from spoiling since there are no refrigerators."

I asked, "Why not cow's milk when there are so many cows running around the marketplace?"

"Those cows you saw are poorly fed and don't give much milk."

For the next three days, we went sightseeing, shopped, ate out, and visited a temple. Wherever Steve and I went, friends and family accompanied us. This required a lot of coordination. Our group was scattered around at different houses, and not all of the houses had telephones. If we didn't decide ahead of time what we were doing, messengers had to be sent to the houses where there were no phones. The day we visited the Red Fort,[6] our group met at Rattan Uncle's house. Once we were all accounted for, the men began flagging down taxis. As each taxi filled up with family and friends, Uncle gave instructions about where to meet at the Red Fort. Steve and I left in the last taxi.

Our Ambassador[7] taxi pulled up at the designated Red Fort entrance gate. I got out and saw crowds of people milling around. Many stared at me. There were foreigners in Delhi, but a pregnant foreigner with a large group of Indians must have been unusual. Then I saw Steve's mother and a few familiar faces at the entrance to the Red Fort. Rattan Uncle did a head count and found out that some members of our group were missing. Two men set out to find them. For nearly an hour, we stood in the blazing sun until everyone was located.

While we were waiting, Ama-ji offered me an orange from her purse. Even though we spoke different languages, I sensed her generosity and motherly love.

I remembered the word for orange and said, "*Suntra.*"

To my surprise, Ama-ji shyly said, "Orange."

---

[6] The Red Fort was built in 1657 and was the residence of Mughal Emperors for two hundred years until 1857. Now it has many museums and is a famous tourist attraction.

[7] Ambassador cars were manufactured by Hindustan Motors of India from 1958 to 2014; they were based on the Morris Oxford series III model and were considered an important status symbol. Most people could not afford a car, but many Ambassadors were used as taxis.

Once everybody was collected at the Red Fort entrance, there was lots of loud talk in Hindi. I guessed that they were arguing about plans. They finally decided that we'd make a quick round of the fort and then go shopping.

After a quick round of the Red Fort, we set out to shop at Chandni Chowk Bazaar, a popular shopping area with reasonable prices. The congested streets were lined with cloth shops. The fronts of the shops had no windows or walls. Colorful saris and cloth pieces hung in the storefronts. As our procession of family and friends walked down the street, we were often stopped by beggars, who became part of the procession even though the men in our party tried to shoo them away. The shopkeepers called out in Hindi, "Please come in our shop; we have beautiful cloth."

Rattan Uncle directed us to his favorite shop. There wasn't enough room for our group of thirty-plus, so some members went into nearby shops. I sat down on a long bench that ran the length of the store. Shelved on the walls of the shop were bolts of cloth in every imaginable color. A heavy-set man in a white *kurta pyjama* (a long shirt with a high collar worn over Indian pajamas) sat cross-legged on a platform, which was covered with a sheet. My mother-in-law and the shopkeeper began to talk in Hindi. She pointed to a bolt of sari cloth. The cloth merchant took the bolt from the shelf and threw it towards the back of the store while holding the loose end of the cloth. Six yards of pink silk gracefully unfolded in front of us. The shopkeeper continued showing us saris until the platform was covered with yards and yards of silk cloth.

Then the shopkeeper motioned to me, indicating that I should touch the silk. It felt like baby skin. He asked me to choose a sari. All were beautiful, and finally I chose a light blue sari with an embroidered border in pastel colors. As soon as I indicated the blue sari, the shopkeeper announced a price of four hundred rupees.[8]

Everyone looked shocked. Ama-ji and Anjana began bargaining with the shopkeeper. Steve explained that the shopkeeper was charging an outrageous price because I was a foreigner. After much haggling, the price was reduced by half, a much more reasonable amount.

We left the shop and went to several similar shops. If a shopkeeper refused to lower his inflated prices, we walked out. Apparently my

---

[8] About thirty-five dollars at that time (all conversions in footnotes are for that time period).

presence in the group was a nuisance, at least as far as getting a good price for our purchases. The shopkeepers thought they had a rich foreign customer who would pay outlandish prices. I was a foreigner, but fortunately my husband's family knew what the standard prices should be.

The next day Steve's sister Vidya asked me to try on one of my new saris. I went to the bedroom and spent twenty minutes trying to drape the sari so it looked good. In the United States, I had worn a sari a couple of times. Each time, my neighbor had helped me put it on. Now with the heat and my protruding stomach, I had difficulty draping the six yards of cloth by myself.

When I finally got the sari fixed as well as I could, I looked at myself in the mirror and felt very sloppy compared to the Indian women, who wore their saris so effortlessly. I was reluctant to show my in-laws, because I expected that they might laugh at me. My petticoat showed below the sari in the front, and the back of the sari dragged on the floor. Much to my surprise, when I reached the living room, I received approval instead of laughter.

Middle sister-in-law Anjana said in Hindi, "You look beautiful."

I thanked her, but I was still sure she was just trying to be polite. I returned to my room and changed back into my American skirt and maternity top. The sari seemed much too dressy to wear around the house. When I came back into the living room in my American clothes, everyone looked disappointed.

Eldest sister-in-law Vidya asked in Hindi, "Why did you change?"

Youngest sister-in-law Hansa added in English, "You look so much prettier in the sari than in your American clothes."

I explained that I was saving the sari for a special occasion.

Hansa said, "We thought you didn't like the sari."

I assured her that I liked the sari, but I got the feeling she didn't believe me.

That evening, Steve's friend Rajinder was giving a dinner party in honor of Steve's return to India and his marriage to me. Everyone who met us at the airport and a few more were invited to the dinner, which was scheduled for nine p.m. Late dinners were one more thing I had to get used to. At eight-thirty, Rajinder picked us up. He was with a young woman, who wore a vibrant green, form-fitting salwar kameez. Rajinder introduced her as a friend from Mandi, Steve's hometown, who was studying in Delhi at Lady Harding Medical College.

Then he asked us, "Can you keep a secret?"

We assured him that we could. He said, "This is my wife, Santosh. We were secretly married last year in a civil ceremony. Our parents told us not to marry until Santosh finished medical college, but we didn't want to wait."

When I heard this, I felt slightly better about the fact that Steve had gone against his parents' wishes.

The four of us reached the restaurant and met up with family and friends. They were seated at long banquet tables, and a four-piece combo was playing Indian and American popular music. We sat at the head table and greeted guests. I studied the menu, saw that all the preparations were Indian dishes, and picked out a few items that sounded familiar.

When the waiter brought the food, it looked greasy. I tasted everything but didn't like anything. There was no resemblance to the Indian food I used to cook in our Durham apartment. My tongue burned from the hot peppers. I couldn't finish any of the food. I wanted a glass of water, but I knew that I shouldn't drink the unboiled water, so I ordered a cup of tea. For dessert, I ordered vanilla ice cream, hoping it might relieve the burning sensation in my mouth. However, the banana taste of the vanilla ice cream was a disappointment. I enjoyed the festive party atmosphere but not the food.

The third day of our stay in Delhi felt hotter than the previous two days. The oppressive heat and constant talk in Hindi was getting to me. There seemed to be an additional current of excitement and loud talk this morning. Steve told me that we were going to an Arya Samaj temple for a religious ceremony.

Hansa instructed me, "You must wear the embroidered maroon silk sari we bought yesterday."

I protested, "I can't wear that heavy sari in this heat. Besides, it's difficult to wrap the sari with my big belly."

Hansa started talking to Madhu in Hindi. I couldn't understand a word of what was said, which only increased my frustration.

Then Steve explained, "You need to wear the fancy sari, because the religious ceremony is especially for us."

I realized that I had no choice in the matter and agreed. I went into the bedroom and struggled to get dressed.

As soon as I was ready, we left for the temple. I was quiet, but there was a lot of noise along the way. Cars and buses honked their horns, drivers shouted at other drivers, and brakes screeched as vehicles stopped for bicycles, cows, and pedestrians on the road.

We arrived at the temple, and family members led us into a large hall. At least forty friends and family members were sitting on the gray-and-white marble floor. Steve and I were guided to the center of the room, where there was a wood fire tended by a man dressed in a long white shirt and a white *dhoti*, a long piece of muslin cloth wrapped around his waist and legs. Steve told me that the man was a *pandit*—a religious person like a church minister—and he was going to perform an *Arya Samaj* ceremony.[9] We joined Steve's sisters and parents, who were sitting in a circle close to the crackling fire and lighting tiny candles. I sat as far from the burning fire as possible. *How could they expect me to sit next to a fire in this sweltering room with just a few fans circulating the hot air?*

Hansa told me to cover my head with the loose end of my sari and be ready to follow instructions. I agreed. "Okay, but please tell me in English what to do."

I recognized that the function was a big deal, especially with so many people sitting cross-legged on the floor intently watching us. I whispered to Steve, "What kind of a ceremony is this?"

He shyly said, "It's our Indian wedding."

Indian wedding at Delhi Arya Samaj Temple.

---

[9] Arya Samaj is a branch of Hindu religion with these principal beliefs: one supreme god, the infallible authority of Vedas (ancient Hindu scriptures), rejection of idol worship, equality of all human beings, and empowerment of women.

We had already been married six months back. I began to sense that Steve's parents felt like the first wedding didn't count. The pandit started reading from a book and then gave us instructions, which I didn't understand, so Steve explained that we had to circle the fire seven times. I led the way, and he held onto the end of my sari while following me. I didn't recognize a word the pandit recited in Sanskrit, a language used in religious ceremonies. During one round of our journey around the blazing fire, I almost tripped over my sari. After three rounds, Steve led the way, and I followed him. Finally, we completed the seven rounds. Then, Steve and I touched the feet of family members in the circle.

There was a lot more activity with the candles and clay containers of oil, but nothing made any sense to me. When the ceremony was over, I was relieved, but I was also upset that I hadn't been explicitly told that the ceremony was going to be our Indian wedding. On the ride back to the house I was quiet, but inside my emotions were in a turmoil.

After four days in Delhi, I felt suffocated by a lack of privacy. I was overwhelmed by a strange language, was constantly surrounded by new people, and was married a second time in six months. I felt the pressure of family members trying to get me to look and act Indian. I sensed that they were trying their best to make me feel comfortable and accepted, but our different languages, customs, and lifestyles were stumbling blocks. I had much to learn in order to make the transition from life in the United States to life in India. My journey would take a long time, with many life-changing challenges along the way.

2
Beginnings

During my first few months in India, I often looked back at the path that had led me here in the first place. Born in New Jersey in 1942, I had moved with my family to Birmingham, Michigan, at age ten. At that time Birmingham was segregated, albeit in a quiet way.[10] Because of this, I had little experience with people of different backgrounds.

After high school I went to Duke University. The undergraduate college was segregated while I was there from 1960 to 1962.[11] There were no black students and no black faculty.

The fall of my freshman year, my dating life was slow. Then a dormmate approached me about a blind date. Before the arrangement, she asked, "Are you okay with dating an Asian Indian graduate student?"

I said, "That's fine."

She added, "He is one of the youngest forestry students, twenty-six years old. Still, there is an age difference of almost seven years."

"It's okay."

This blind date changed my life in a direction I never could have imagined.

My first date with Steve went well. We had an American meal at the Rathskeller in Chapel Hill, North Carolina. We talked a lot on our

---

[10] I later learned that real estate agents had a point system in which they rated prospective buyers. This system eliminated people of certain racial, ethnic, and religious backgrounds, who were told that nothing was available with their requirements.

[11] It wasn't until 1963 that the first black undergraduates enrolled at Duke.

ride home. Steve had an Indian accent but was easy to understand. I really liked him and hoped he felt the same way about me.

A couple days later he called and asked me for a second date. This time he wanted to cook an outdoor meal for me at a picnic spot in the Duke Forest and asked whether I liked barbequed steak. I gladly accepted his offer. We had a great time together, and I realized that he loved cooking and eating. He told me that Indians didn't eat beef, but he had started eating beef when his American friends insisted that he try it.

Steve (Madhu) and Elma grilling in Durham, North Carolina

He continued to ask me out, and we dated steadily for the rest of my freshman year. We played bridge together; visited the Duke Forest,[12] ate at American restaurants; and partied with friends. Sometimes we double-dated with American grad students. Steve was comfortable with them, and they accepted him despite the ever-present racial prejudices of the 1960s.

Elma and Steve in the Duke Forest

We were especially friendly with an Indian married couple who lived in the same house where Steve rented a room. The husband was an engineering graduate student. His wife, Tara, helped me experiment with wearing a sari. She also introduced me to Indian food, which took time getting used to.

---

[12] The Duke Forest was managed by the university and was used for research, teaching, and recreation.

When I went home for spring break, I told my high school friends about Steve. One of them asked me how I felt about dating an Asian man, particularly since almost all of our high school peers had been white Americans. I told her that it felt normal. Except for his slightly darker skin and accent, we had a lot in common. Both of us were family oriented, and we each had three sisters.

After spring break we continued to date. Steve was working hard to finish his forestry PhD thesis, but neither of us liked the idea of being away from each other over the long summer break. He made plans to take a week off from his studies to visit me in Charlevoix, Michigan, where I had a job as a waitress. His July visit to Charlevoix strengthened our relationship, and it was a big letdown for both of us when Steve went back to Durham.

In September we were together again at Duke and dated each other exclusively. That fall, Steve started inviting me to his rented room. Our lovemaking intensified. Shortly after Thanksgiving, it was apparent that I was pregnant. We were quite taken aback by this unplanned news. At first I was upset, but Steve assured me that it was okay. In fact, he wanted to marry me. This helped with my misgivings, but I was worried about how to tell my parents.

When I went home for Christmas vacation, I started by telling my parents that Steve and I wanted to get married. They suggested that I visit India with him before making any commitment. Of course, it was too late for this.

That evening I got my nerve up to reveal my pregnancy to my parents. I decided to talk to them in their bedroom so that my sisters wouldn't hear our conversation. I nervously knocked on their door, and Daddy said, "Come in."

Once in the room, I said in a shaky voice, "I have to tell you why I can't visit India before Steve and I marry. It's too late. I'm pregnant."

Both Mother and Daddy looked shocked. They were upset but did not suggest an abortion, which was something Steve and I didn't want. I said that Steve thought we should get married as soon as I returned to Durham. My parents suggested that we have a church wedding in Birmingham. The wedding date was set for semester break at the First Presbyterian Church. The guest list consisted of close to sixty family members and friends. Steve had Indian friends here in the United States but no Indian relatives.

Steve wrote to his father, *Babu-ji*, explaining that he planned to marry me but omitting any mention of the pregnancy. His father's reply came back in a blue aerogram. The family did not think the marriage was a good idea, since Madhu was already engaged to a woman in his hometown. Steve wrote back that he was definitely marrying me and that the wedding was set for January 27, 1962. Shortly before our marriage, we received a letter from Babu-ji saying that the family accepted the marriage and that I was welcome into the family.

Right before the wedding, Steve and I met with Dr. Harris, the minister at the church. He talked about marriage vows. He emphasized that marriage was a long-term commitment and that it was important for couples to live within their income.

For our church wedding, I wore a simple, knee-length, white wedding dress, and Steve wore a navy-blue suit. I didn't think I looked pregnant. We hadn't told anybody except my parents about the pregnancy.

The day of the wedding was extremely cold, and the ground was covered with snow. Out-of-town guests stayed at the homes of friends in the neighborhood. My college roommate, Martha, was my maid of honor; my sister Barbara was the flower girl; and Steve's friend George Dheer, an Indian graduate student, was his best man.

Elma and Steve's wedding in Birmingham, Michigan

Our reception was a catered dinner at my parents' home. Following the reception, we went on a two-day honeymoon and then returned to Durham. I shifted from my dorm room to Steve's apartment and continued with my sophomore classes as a part-time student. Steve was in the final stage of his thesis work and expected to graduate in June. Time flew for us. We juggled classes, exams, doctor appointments, thesis work, Steve's job search, and decisions about moving to India.

Two and a half months after our marriage, my pregnancy started to show, so we began telling friends. At that time, Steve wrote his father and told him about the pregnancy. His father wrote back that the family was delighted. He continued to ask Madhu to return to India and bring me with him. Steve was the only son, and his parents expected him to be in India to care for them. Steve felt we needed to go to India and try living there. His father assured him that he would get a job in the Himachal Pradesh Forestry Department soon after his arrival.

At first, I was uncomfortable about the idea of moving to India. Steve was well-accepted in the United States, even with the racial discrimination in the 1960s. I wondered how I would be accepted in India and asked Steve if there were any Americans in his hometown. He admitted there were none. It seemed to me that living in the United States was a better plan. I suggested that Steve apply for a job here and think about going to India after the birth of our child. He reluctantly applied for a couple of jobs in the United States and Canada but continued to persuade me that we should try living in India. After many discussions, I agreed to make the trip to India in June.

As June arrived, Steve was busy with graduation activities. It was his second Duke University graduation. In 1958 he had received his Master of Forestry. Now he was to receive a Doctorate in Forestry. I was busy with my second-year exams. In between studying and taking exams, I was packing our belongings for storage and shipment to India.

Elma with Steve at his Duke PhD graduation

When graduation, and packing were finally behind us, we flew to Michigan for a short visit with my family. Before I knew it, I was saying goodbye to my parents and younger sisters at the Detroit Metropolitan Airport. The anxiety about the trip to India hadn't caught up with me yet. It wasn't until we boarded the Air India Boeing 707 that I realized I had no idea when I would see my family again or what was ahead.

Shimla: A Long Wait for a Job

After our initial four days in Delhi, Steve's immediate family joined us on a twelve-hour trip to Shimla, where some of them lived. Steve planned to apply for a job with the Himachal Pradesh Forest Service in Shimla. He was excited about his new life but also anxious about the uncertain future. He had left India at age nineteen as a student and returned in the new roles of husband, father-to-be, and—hopefully—Indian forest official.

From Delhi to Shimla—Babu-ji, Ama-ji, Steve's sisters, an uncle, and his middle sister's family travelled with us. The trip began with an overnight train ride from Delhi to Kalka and then shifted to a Himachal Pradesh transport bus for the five-hour ride from Kalka to Shimla, where the family had made plans for us to stay at his sister Anjana's home. As the bus climbed the hilly road, a cool breeze came through the open windows. Not so pleasant was the dust that entered with the breeze. Once again, my American maternity top and skirt looked out of place. The Indian passengers stared at me. My in-laws had warned me that I would probably be the only foreigner on the bus, and they were right. They had suggested that I wear one of the saris we bought in Delhi, but I felt the beautiful saris were for parties and not for traveling.

It was a relief to have some downtime on the bus ride after rushing around Delhi for sightseeing, eating out, shopping, and our Indian marriage ceremony. Being bombarded with a strange language and unfamiliar customs was overwhelming. As much as I had prepared for our move from the United States to India, during those first four days I was constantly surprised and shocked by my new life.

During the ride, Steve and I talked about the job application process. Babu-ji had assured us that there was a job available with the Himachal Pradesh Forest Department. His friends in senior government positions had talked with the Chief Conservator of Forests and were told that Madhu was a good fit for the position.

I asked Steve, "How long do you think the hiring process will take?"

"It's hard to say. I'm out of touch with the Indian system. Hopefully, I'll get the job within a month. I know you want us to be on our own."

Steve was accustomed to being surrounded by family members. I wanted to meet everyone but needed my own space. Most important, I wanted Steve to secure his new job before we had our baby. The due date was the first week of September, which didn't give us much time.

Finally, we reached the crowded Shimla bus terminal. I couldn't believe the refreshing cool air. It was heaven after Delhi's sweltering heat. People stared at me, but already I was getting used to being stared at. Tilak *Mama* (Uncle) arranged several jeeps to take us to Anjana's house, and we left for the Longwood area of Shimla. After a mile on Cart Road, we came to a sharp curve and turned up a steep road. The jeeps stopped in front of a metal gate.

We all got out and walked down a footpath to Anjana's house. An aunt greeted us at the door. She was taking care of *Bari Mata-ji*, respected grandmother, who was too old and frail to make the trip to Delhi. I was directed into a small, dimly lit room, where Bari Mata-ji sat cross-legged on a bed reading a religious book. I said, "Namaste-ji" and respectfully touched her feet. She smiled and gently put her hand on my shoulder.

Anjana and her husband insisted on giving us their bedroom for our stay. They knew we needed the privacy. Recently married, we would have found it hard to be apart at night.

Anjana's house was adequate for her family, but with an average of eight guests, the house was always crowded with relatives and friends who came to meet me and to see Steve again after six years. It seemed that whenever one set of relatives left, a new group arrived. Most of the guests slept dormitory-style in the living room. More people slept on the floor than in beds. During the day, all the bedding in the living room was stacked in the tiny, dark bedroom that everyone had to walk through to get to the bathroom, which had four commodes, wooden chairs with chamber pots covered by lids. The lack of a flush toilet took time to get used to.

During our first weeks at Shimla, we often went on pleasure trips to the town. Steve was also busy with visits to the forest department office, which was part of the government headquarters at Shimla. He interviewed for the job and submitted the required paperwork for his application. Now we had to wait and see.

I loved our outings to the Shimla bazaar. During the British rule in India, Shimla was the summer capital of India from 1864 until shortly before the British left India in 1947. The architecture and layout of the town retained its British influence. The center of town was a forty-five minute hike from the house. Once there, Steve and I walked up and down Mall Road, greeted friends, and had tea in one of the many restaurants.

Shimla Mall

Mall Road was a hub of activity, with people visiting the Gaiety Theater, Municipal Corporation Office, General Post Office, Scandal Point,[13] shops, and hotels. Although Mall Road was for pedestrians only, occasionally an ambulance or a car with a top government official

---

[13] Scandal Point is at the junction of Mall Road and Ridge Road. The name came from the supposed elopement of the daughter of a British Viceroy and an Indian Maharajah.

plied the road. One day we saw a black Ambassador car drive by with a flag on it. Steve said, "I think I see the governor in the car." On the way home we stopped at The Ridge,[14] sat on wooden benches, and looked up at the historical Christ Church.

I also loved the beautiful mountain views from the town of Shimla. At 7,000 feet above sea level, the cool climate was very comfortable.

During the monsoons, however, daily walks weren't always possible. As June turned into July, I frequently found myself cooped up in the two-bedroom house with at least ten other family members. With an overabundance of free time, a lack of concrete language skills, and few daily responsibilities, I worried even more about the future.

---

[14] The Ridge is a large open space that is centrally located. It is used for cultural programs, fairs, and government functions.

4

Tough Times

Three months had passed since we landed in India, and we were still waiting for Steve to get his forestry job. So many things were bothering me. Usually, I'm a pretty positive person. Was it because of being pregnant? Would life in India get better? I certainly hoped so.

I was desperate for our own place and some privacy, and at times I longed for America. I still couldn't eat much of the Indian food, and I hungered for my favorite American dishes, like cheesecake, spaghetti and meatballs, steak, and mashed potatoes. Of course, steak was out of the question. Hindus didn't eat beef, and it wasn't available in any of the meat shops.

One day, I thought I'd try to make mashed potatoes to cheer myself up. I ventured into the kitchen and surveyed the possibilities for cooking. Anjana's kitchen consisted of two side-by-side, small, dimly lit rooms. Both had gray cement floors and smoke-stained walls. The first room had a small wooden table with shelves above it. There were brass cooking pans lined upside down on the shelves. The second room had a single-burner, brass kerosene stove on the floor, a charcoal fireplace for cooking along the back wall, and a door that led outside. As I entered the second room, Ama-ji looked up from her cooking and pointed frantically. Anjana rushed over and started to lead me out of the kitchen.

Before I was shooed out, I noticed my mother-in-law's bare legs. Her *salwar*, a pair of pajama-like pants, was lying on the floor. Yet she didn't rush over to put them on when she saw me. Instead, she remained squatting, and I could see that she was busy opening the pressure cooker on the kerosene stove. It all seemed very strange to me.

There was no time for questions. In a loud, authoritative voice Anjana said, "Elma, leave the kitchen!" Anjana didn't usually speak English, but it was clear that she desperately needed me to follow her instructions. I left the kitchen, wondering why I wasn't welcome.

In the front hallway, which was also the dining room, I sat down at the table feeling confused and upset. Babu-ji, who was sitting there, saw that I was disturbed. He asked Anjana, "What's the problem?"

She started speaking in Hindi. After she finished, Babu-ji began to explain what all the commotion was about. "Ama-ji is cooking food for my mother. When she makes rice and lentils, there are certain Mandi customs that must be strictly followed for widows." Then, he told me that no one could touch the food while it was being cooked if they had a *salwar* or pants on.

I later learned that Ama-ji did all the cooking for her mother-in-law, Bari Mata-ji, whose diet and food preparation had changed drastically when her husband, a forest contractor, died. Widows did not eat meat, garlic, or onions. It was thought that these items increased their sexual appetites. No meat—and other food restrictions—were common throughout India, but the process followed in Mandi to cook rice and lentils for a widow, including the removal of the pants, was quite different. After this incident, I stayed out of Anjana's kitchen and gave up on trying to cook American food.

As I spent more time with Steve's family, my great respect for both Ama-ji and Babu-ji continued to grow. Babu-ji was highly regarded by family, friends, and colleagues. The year before, he had retired from his senior post of Sessions Court Judge in the state judiciary system. Before his retirement, he had lived in Shimla in a huge, single-family government house that was staffed with many servants to cook, clean, and run errands. However, all of these perks had ended with his retirement. Since that time, he had been living with Ama-ji and his mother, Bari Mata-ji, in his ancestral home in Mandi, Himachal Pradesh. Now he was back in Shimla for a few months to be with us and to expedite the securing of the promised forestry job for his only son.

This wait for the job was a major cause of anxiety for all of us. Whenever Babu-ji and I talked about the hurdles that came up in the job application process, he appeared apprehensive, which was not typical of his usual calm demeanor. As time progressed, his loose-fitting pants seemed to hang on him, and I'm sure the delay was the cause of his weight loss.

The effects of this stress came to a head two days after the kitchen incident, when Babu-ji became upset with me and Steve. We had gone out with a group of Steve's high school classmates for an evening meal at Davico's, a fancy restaurant on the Mall Road that had a live band that played both Indian and Western music. As usual, I couldn't eat much except for a few appetizers. After dinner we walked the two miles home, returning at about ten-thirty.

Steve and I quietly entered the house, trying not to disturb anyone. But as soon as we walked into the living room, where most of the family was sleeping, Babu-ji spoke up. "Why are you so late? We were worried about you. You shouldn't stay out so late!"

I was shocked by his reprimands. It was only ten-thirty, and Steve and I were out together. As a high school teenager in Michigan in the late 1950s, I had enjoyed more freedom than I possessed in India as a twenty-year-old, married woman. Steve apologized for being late, and we quickly went into our bedroom. I wished Steve would get the promised job so that we could have our own home and some of the freedoms I was used to.

Another big problem for me was the language. There were so many discussions in Hindi that I didn't understand because I could only follow simple conversations. Friends and family members spoke to me in English as long as everyone in the group spoke English, but as soon as a non-English-speaking person joined our group, the conversation switched to Hindi.

One afternoon, Steve's sister Hansa was talking to me in the front hall. She questioned why I resisted wearing Indian clothes and didn't try harder to eat the Indian food. She said that she knew of some visiting foreigners who were quick to wear Indian clothes and eat traditional dishes. I tried to explain that such an adaptation to the lifestyle was probably easier for people who knew that they would be here for a short time and that the changes were temporary. In contrast, I knew I was here for the long haul and felt like I couldn't pretend that I was comfortable in the clothes or liked the food.

Before we could finish our discussion, we were called into the living room, where family members were conversing in Hindi and listening to Hindi music on the radio.[15] As soon as we entered the room, Han-

---

[15] There were no televisions in India during the 1960s.

sa started speaking Hindi with the rest of the family. I recognized a few words, *kapray* (clothes) and *khanna* (food). *Kapray, kapray, kapray, khanna, khanna, khanna*—why were they always talking about food and clothes? Several family members were speaking loudly at the same time, and the volume was competing with the loud Hindi film songs playing on the radio. It was too much for me. I left the room, went into our bedroom, got in bed, and pulled the heavy quilt over my head. My eardrums were ringing and pounding from the constant barrage of loud, foreign sounds, and I longed for silence.

5

Babu-ji

Despite the moments of frustration, during the four months we lived at Anjana's home I looked forward to my daily interactions with my father-in-law, Babu-ji. From him, I learned so much about Mandi customs, my in-laws, Himachal Pradesh government, and much more. Most important, I enjoyed Babu-ji's shy smile and his warm, compassionate, humble personality.

One afternoon, bright sunshine warmed the enclosed porch, a long, narrow room with wide-planked, rough wooden floors and windows that ran the full length of the room. The sunshine was a welcome relief after three days of Shimla monsoon rains. Babu-ji and I sat drinking our afternoon tea in the porch, which also served as a dining room. Teatime with Babu-ji was special for two reasons: the food served with tea and the conversations in English.

While I found most Indian meals to be far too spicy, I thoroughly enjoyed the teatime offerings. These typically included buttered toast, French fries, cashew nuts, and biscuits (cookies). Occasionally, I had a hardboiled egg. Babu-ji was a strict vegetarian, but he did not mind if I ate eggs or meat.

Even better than the food was the one-on-one time Babu-ji and I had together. When no other family members joined us, our conversations remained in English. Babu-ji spoke English fluently with an Indian-English accent.

We talked about Indian customs, politics, Shimla history, the judiciary system, and Madhu's job application. More comfortable topics for Babu-ji concerned his family and hometown of Mandi in Himachal Pradesh. The town was located in the Beas River valley, 3,000 feet above sea level, and surrounded by high mountains on all sides. Babu-ji grew up in Mandi, went to law school in Lahore, worked in many Himachal Pradesh towns, and returned to live in Mandi after his retirement in 1961.

Babu-ji, who often wore a Nehru-collared gray shirt that matched his graying hair, frequently talked about how much he loved his extended family and how he had cared for them. He told me, "My father's brother, who lived in our ancestral house, died at a young age, leaving behind his wife and five children."

"How did you help them?"

"I helped financially with household expenses, was involved in my three nephews' and two nieces' education, and assisted in arranging their marriages."

If I hadn't asked, I don't think Babu-ji would have explained how much he had helped. Even while answering my questions, I think he was being conservative about how much he did for these family members.

On a different afternoon we talked about marriages. I said, "My marriage must have been a shock for you and the family."

He was quiet for a few minutes and then replied, "Yes, it was difficult for me when I read Madhu's letter saying he planned to marry an American that he'd met at Duke. I wrote back, 'You should rethink this marriage, especially since you are engaged to a Mandi woman of the same caste.' When Madhu replied that he definitely planned to marry you, I sent my letter accepting the decision."

"It must have been hard for you to tell the woman's family that the six-year engagement had to be broken and why."

Ama-ji and Babu-ji

He revealed, "It was one of the most difficult times in my life."

"Thank you for being so tolerant."

I realized that even though it was tough for him and the rest of my in-laws to accept me with so many differences in our cultures, they truly had welcomed me into the family.

I asked Babu-ji about his marriage. He told me, "Marriages in India are arranged within the same caste by the parents. In Mandi they go further by focusing on finding a suitable match within the town." He went on to explain that his marriage was arranged with Ama-ji when they were very young. Both were of the same caste, *Kshatriya*.[16] Their families lived less than a mile apart. When Babu-ji talked about his arranged marriage, he never called Ama-ji by her first name, Sarla. He always called her Ama-ji or Madhu's mother.

Babu-ji said, "I was married at age fourteen, and Ama-ji was seven."

I asked, "Was it common for people to marry at such a young age?"

"Yes, it was. At first Ama-ji stayed at her parents' home and came to our home during the day. She was home-schooled while visiting. I finished college in Mandi and then attended law school in Lahore."

I wanted to ask him when he and Ama-ji started to live together, but I was embarrassed to question him.[17]

Babu-ji talked about his desire to work for the government rather than be a private lawyer. He told me, "I began my job search by taking the Punjab judiciary exam."[18]

After the results were announced, he was offered a position in the Punjab Judiciary Department. He said, "My mother, Bari Mata-ji, told me that I shouldn't leave Mandi to work in Punjab and should wait for a job offer closer to home. I accepted her advice and didn't make the move."

He was not in the habit of disagreeing with his mother. In fact, I later learned that his eldest daughter, Vidya, had entered an inappropriate marriage because Bari Mata-ji insisted that they honor the engagement, even after Ama-ji protested vehemently and asked to call it off when it was learned that the man was mentally challenged and had many issues. Then, after the marriage, Bari Mata-ji did not want them to get a divorce. Babu-ji accepted his mother's wishes, so even though Vidya and her husband lived apart for more than twenty years, they divorced only after Bari Mata-ji died.

Babu-ji went on to tell me about his career in government service. He said, "Soon after I refused the Punjab position, I was hired as a magistrate in Mandi State. Even with discrimination against Kshatriyas in Mandi State, I did get the position. I was the only qualified judge in my home state."

---

[16] Second highest status in the four social classes, traditionally military or ruling class.

[17] I did ask Madhu's younger sister, Hansa, at a later time. She told me that they didn't live as husband and wife until Babu-ji completed his law degree, returned to Mandi, and started looking for work.

[18] Recently, my brother-in-law told me that Babu-ji received top scores on the exam. This is something Babu-ji would have been too modest to tell me on his own.

I was a little surprised when he mentioned this. Self-praise was not his mode. He continued, "When Himachal Pradesh was established as a Chief Commissioner's Province within the Union of India in 1948, I was hired as District Sessions Judge and served as judge for the whole state of Himachal. My headquarters shifted every three months to the different district headquarters. As the workload increased, a second Sessions Judge was hired. Most of the time I worked in Shimla but went on tour to Rohru, Rampur, and Nahan when there were cases for me to preside over. I lived in Shimla until my retirement in 1961."

Babu-ji said, "I seriously considered the offer of extending my service but felt family obligations and my health were more important than the job. I decided to retire at the usual age of fifty-five, having completed almost thirty years of service. I have no regrets."[19]

Another day at teatime, it was raining heavily, and the porch felt chilly. Babu-ji was wearing a beige, hand-knit sweater with a dark brown Nehru jacket. Normally after tea, he played bridge with friends at the club on the Shimla Mall, but today he didn't want to walk in the rain. Babu-ji said, "If we had a phone, I'd call my friend Lala Hem Chand, who used to work with me, and ask him to come play bridge here."

Right after Babu-ji mentioned this, there was a knock at the front door. My sister-in-law Anjana admitted a young boy dressed in rain-soaked pajamas and a *kurtha*. The boy had a message from his boss, Lala Hem Chand, asking whether we'd like to play bridge at home. Babu-ji told the servant to have his boss come over. I was excited about playing bridge because Madhu and I loved the card game. We had played in many college tournaments at Duke.

After an hour, Hem Chand, who lived about six houses down the road, arrived to play bridge. He took his shoes off after entering the front door.

Babu-ji said, "Thank you for coming over in the rain, and how is your mother?"

Hem Chand answered, "I didn't mind the rain, but the steep road was slippery and muddy. My mother is fine but misses Mandi. How is yours?"

---

[19] My brother-in-law told me more about Babu-ji's career. Before Babu-ji's retirement he was the senior-most Sessions Judge in the country and was offered an extension in his service. If he had taken it, he probably would have become Judicial Commissioner and might have been selected for the Supreme Court.

"Bari Mata-ji is fine, but she also misses her Mandi friends and relatives."

Once in the living room, Hem Chand asked me, "When did you start playing bridge?"

"I started playing when I was in middle school and started teaching my friends in high school in weekly classes at a friend's home."

Babu-ji added, "I've been playing since I was in college. Enough talk, let's start our bridge game. Madhu and Elma will begin as partners since they both follow Goren bidding conventions. Hem Chand and I will play together, since we use Indian conventions. After a few games, we can change partners."

Our occasional bridge games became an added special treat to our afternoon teatime.

Special Delivery at Snowdon Hospital

During my first two months of living at Shimla, I made three visits to a maternity clinic for women who planned to deliver at the Snowdon Government Hospital. The staff was knowledgeable and friendly. I got more attention here than I had ever received at my doctor appointments in North Carolina. All the patients in the clinic were Indian women so I was a novelty. Most of the staff spoke English, which was reassuring since I hardly understood Hindi.

The clinic was between Lakhar Bazaar, a group of small shops that sold wooden artifacts, and Snowdon Hospital, the largest and best hospital in the state of Himachal Pradesh. Getting to the clinic involved a half-hour, hilly walk from my sister-in-law's bungalow. For my first two clinic visits, I was accompanied by two female family members. Since I felt comfortable with the route and liked doing things on my own, I wanted to make the next visit by myself.

I asked Steve to get permission from his family for me to go on my own. He asked his family, and they reluctantly agreed that I would be allowed if Madhu walked with me as far as Lakhar Bazaar. This freedom was pretty special. We started off together. Once we reached Lakhar Bazaar, he sent me alone on a straight road to the clinic. When I got there, I learned more about my hospital stay and delivery. However, the staff said they were saving detailed information for my next scheduled visit, which would be in two weeks, the end of August.

Special Delivery at Snowdon Hospital

I woke up the next morning with abdominal pains. I tried to convince myself that they were caused by something I ate. I tried to go back to sleep, but the pains continued. They really hurt. I thought, *These can't be labor pains; it's too soon.*

When the pains didn't stop, I woke Steve up. He didn't know what to do and thought we should wake Ama-ji and Anjana. I wanted to wait a little longer, hoping that the pains would subside. A month earlier, I had experienced false labor pains. However, as time progressed, this started to feel more and more like it could be the real thing.

We woke the family. When the pains got more intense, Ama-ji and Anjana decided that we needed to go to the hospital. They sent a message to my youngest sister-in-law, who lived close by, asking her to send a vehicle. While waiting, I packed an overnight bag, and a servant packed a bedroll with assorted bedding.

When the jeep station wagon arrived, several family members crowded into the jeep with me and Steve, while the rest followed on foot. The ride to the hospital, which followed the forested, hilly back road that wound up to the hospital on the Sanjauli side of Shimla, took twenty-five minutes. As my pains intensified, it seemed like forever.

When we reached the hospital entrance gate, a man in uniform stopped us, and our driver shouted out in Hindi, "American lady in the jeep; baby about to be born; let us go!"

On hearing that there was a pregnant foreigner in the jeep, the gatekeeper let us pass and pointed to the entrance that led to the delivery room. We drove to the door and rushed inside. Anjana and her husband, Ishwar-ji, led the way. We arrived at a desk, and the staff started to ask questions. They soon realized that I needed to get to the delivery room quickly.

While Steve and the men stayed behind to finish the paperwork, a white uniformed nurse asked me to lie down on a stretcher. I wanted to walk, but she insisted that I get on the stretcher. With all the confusion of Hindi directions, translations, and broken English, I gave in and obeyed her instructions. Two orderlies carried me on the stretcher toward the delivery room, and the women in the family followed me.

When we arrived in the delivery room, I was reassured to see my favorite nurse and lady doctor. In less than two hours, I was looking at my newborn baby boy.

Ama-ji smiled at me and said, *"Aap ne bahut accha kya. Hamara bahut sundar larka hai."*

A nurse translated, saying, "You did very well. We have a beautiful boy."

I kept looking at my little miracle and then asked to see Madhu. They told me that I could see him when I was in the recovery room. The lady doctor noticed I was upset by the delay, so she said that he could come into the delivery room after everything was cleaned up. Once the staff was ready, they allowed Madhu into the delivery room. He shyly stopped a few feet from me and our little baby boy, who was lying next to me. Both of us were speechless as we looked at our precious newborn and each other.

Finally Steve said, "How are you and the baby?"

I could hardly say anything. Seeing Steve and hearing his voice, I was overcome with emotion. The lady doctor spoke up. "They both are doing extremely well, but your wife needs some rest."

She added that Madhu should leave and come up to the maternity ward in an hour.

After more checking of vitals, Ama-ji, baby, and I were ready to go to our room. Once again, I was taken on a stretcher, and our little one was carried by a nurse. We passed through several corridors, and then they carried me up the stairs on the stretcher, which was quite scary. Finally we reached our room, which was at the end of a long, dark hallway. As we entered the room, I was surprised at how large and bright it was. I noticed two adult hospital beds but no baby bed.

A nurse helped me into a chair and asked if I wanted to hold my baby while I waited for the bed to be made up.

I said, "I'd love to, but where is the baby's bed?"

The nurse seemed surprised. "I don't think we have one. All our babies sleep in bed with their mothers."

I could see that things were going to be different during my hospital stay. Then she said, "Oh, maybe I can get a baby bed from the children's ward."

She left the room to check and returned with a bassinet that looked just right.

Then I asked, "Will another patient be using the other bed in the room?"

The nurse replied, "No, it's for one of your family members."

I thought, *Oh, that's perfect. Steve can be my attendant, and we will have some private time.*

Special Delivery at Snowdon Hospital

My mother-in-law sat on the bed, and we waited for our bedding to be brought up from the jeep. The luggage arrived, the beds were made up, and I asked for Madhu.

A nurse said, "It's another half hour before visiting hours start, and then he can come to the room, but only during visiting hours."

I was upset by this rule. The nurse added, "The hospital is *very* strict about honoring women's privacy."

Finally, Steve walked into the room with Ishwar-ji and my father-in-law, Babu-ji. Both the baby and I were in our own beds resting. I sat up and tried to understand the conversation. Occasionally, I heard an English word in the loud discussions. I guessed that they were talking about the baby bassinet and *khanna*, food. So far, Steve hadn't spoken to me, except when he formally asked me how I was doing. I wished he'd come closer and give our baby and me a kiss, but I knew that Indian culture frowned upon males and females kissing in public, not even married couples.

I asked Steve, "What is this privacy rule about not allowing males in the room except during visiting hours? I want you to stay in the room as my attendant."

Steve wasn't familiar with these rules, having been in the United States for the last six years. He tried to reassure me, saying, "I'll talk to the administrator of the hospital. He studied abroad, and I'm sure he'll make an exception for us."

While we were talking, the lady doctor who had delivered our baby, several white-uniformed staff members, and an authoritative-looking male figure entered the room. My doctor introduced us to the unfamiliar male, who was the hospital administrator and also a doctor. We conversed comfortably in English. After a friendly discussion, Steve and I brought up our request to allow him to stay in the hospital room throughout the day and night.

The administrator explained, "Our rules do not permit this. We are in India, and not in an American hospital. Female patients would be very uncomfortable with a male in the maternity ward."

We argued that Madhu would stay inside our private room so no one would be inconvenienced.

He repeated, "I understand this might not be a problem in an American hospital, but here it's a problem."

I tried to explain. "I don't know Hindi, and my mother-in-law, who is the designated attendant, doesn't know English."

Finally, the head doctor agreed to let Madhu stay throughout the day with me, but he wasn't allowed to spend the night. I realized that this was the best arrangement we were going to get and further arguments would be useless. This meant that Ama-ji would be my overnight attendant.

A hungry cry came from our little baby, and my mother-in-law handed him to me. My milk hadn't come in yet, but I kept trying to nurse him. Steve looked lovingly at our son and said, "I feel bad that they won't bend the hospital rules."

"It's okay. Let's think about a name for our little one."

Steve hesitated and then said that we couldn't choose a name until the naming ceremony, which would be the thirteenth day after the delivery. The name had to start with a certain *akshar*, letter. The letter would be decided by a *pandit*, a religious leader like the one who had performed our second wedding ceremony. This meant I had to keep calling our little one "baby boy" or think of a temporary nickname. I realized again that so many things were out of my control. If we had been in the United States, Steve and I would have chosen the name ourselves before leaving the hospital.

No baby's name for thirteen days, no husband as attendant, and no one to speak English with during the nights proved to be quite a challenge. Communication with my mother-in-law was creative, full of gestures, and sometimes humorous as we struggled to understand each other. She spoke slowly, using single words when possible, and pointed at things to help me understand. I tried using a few Hindi words that I had learned. Sometimes I understood a word, like *bacha*, because she would point to our baby.

Often my pronunciation was so poor that Ama-ji had no idea what I was saying. During one of our conversations, I kept repeating, "*Bhookh, bhookh, bhookh.*" ("Hungry, hungry, hungry.") Ama-ji smiled, shook her head to acknowledge me, and acted like she understood, but when she took no further action, I knew that she did not. I tried to convey that I wanted her to heat up some of the leftover food from home. We didn't eat the hospital food, but we had fresh food that was prepared and delivered by family members. However, Ama-ji didn't have her breakfast before eleven. I liked to eat early, so I asked her for breakfast immediately after our morning chai. I kept saying, "*Bhookh, bhookh, bhookh.*" Each time, Ama-ji nodded in assent but did nothing.

Finally, she smiled and pantomimed reading a book. I started laughing when I realized that she thought I was saying the English word *book*. She still didn't get it, but finally a nurse walked into the room. I explained the scene to the nurse, who translated for Ama-ji. As soon as Ama-ji understood, she also laughed at our miscommunication.

I told the nurse that this conversation started because I wanted breakfast. Then the nurse translated that the family would be bringing fresh food but not for a couple of hours. She offered to get me breakfast from the hospital kitchen. At first, Ama-ji said *no* to the hospital food, but eventually the nurse convinced Ama-ji that the hospital food was safe for me to eat.

I asked the nurse, "Does the kitchen have toast and a hardboiled egg?"

She said, "That's easy" and returned quickly with my request. I had my breakfast and wondered why I wasn't allowed to eat hospital fare. The nurse told me that Ama-ji worried that the hospital food might be spoiled, because it wasn't refrigerated. There were only a few refrigerators in the hospital, and they were used for storing medicine.

My expected three-day stay in the hospital extended to a week. Getting the nursing worked out for the first time wasn't easy. My breasts got swollen, and I developed a fever. It didn't last long once my breasts were pumped, and Baby Boy and Mom soon figured out breastfeeding. Still, my doctor said that I needed to extend my hospital stay. She was afraid that I might get sick at home and have to be readmitted.

Now that the breastfeeding was going smoothly, I wanted to go home to my bedroom so I could finally be alone with husband and baby. I wanted to put my own baby-rearing experiences in place, and I hoped to figure out a substitute for the Indian diapers, which involved a single thin, triangular cloth that tied in front. I was still waiting for the American diapers to arrive by ship with the rest of our belongings from North Carolina. In the meantime, the Indian diapers didn't work well, and we were constantly changing the baby's clothes and the bedding in the bassinet.

As much as I liked the attention of the hospital staff and enjoyed the large, clean room, which had an attached bathroom with a flush toilet and was much better than our shared commode system at home, I wanted out of Snowdon Hospital. Of course, I had no say in the matter. Finally, on the seventh day of my hospital stay, my lady doctor came into the room and gave her okay for me to go home.

Paperwork was completed, and we prepared to leave. Bedding,

clothes, a kerosene stove, three *tiffans* (stacked stainless steel containers for carrying food), and other miscellaneous items were packed to take home. Staff members kept coming to our room to say goodbye. There were a few tears shed by nurses, assistant nurses, Ama-ji, and me. At last we were ready to go. With the help of family members and hospital staff, our belongings followed us down to the waiting jeep. Off to home and a new chapter in Indian baby-rearing.

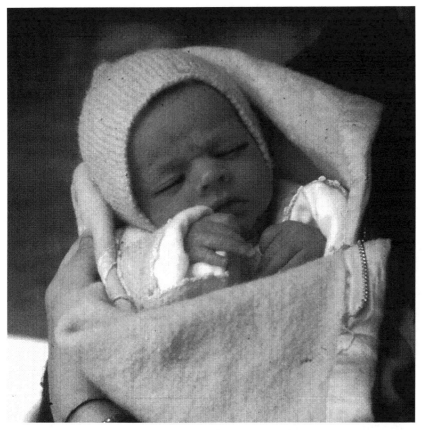

Baby Raju

7

Job Celebration

About six weeks later, I heard a familiar cough outside my sister-in-law Anjana's home and knew Steve was back from his visit to the forestry office. With many questions, I hurried to meet him. As the door opened, I felt the cold autumn air rush into the entrance hallway. It was now October of 1962—almost four months since we had arrived in India from the United States.

Steve quickly closed the door behind him and didn't say a word. I asked apprehensively, "When do you start work?"

Steve smiled and said, "As soon as we can get ready to leave."

Before I had a chance to ask what he meant, my in-laws joined us. The women came from the kitchen. The children burst in through the front door, slamming it behind them. The men stopped their game of rummy on the dining room table and brought their chairs over to the group gathered in the middle of the room. Steve's father, Babu-ji, came in from the living room, where he had been reading *The Tribune*, an English edition of an Indian newspaper published in Chandigarh.

The last person to enter the room was Steve's grandmother, Bari Mata-ji. Her thinning, black hair was streaked with gray and pulled back from her wrinkled face in a small bun. She weighed about eighty pounds and was shorter than five feet. She was late to arrive because she needed to finish her prayers. Most of her day was spent praying and reading religious books. She was the oldest and most respected family member.

Everybody talked at once. Sisters, uncles, aunts, cousins, nephews, and parents kept asking Madhu questions. Since I was outnumbered, the loud conversation continued in *Mandiali*, the dialect of Hindi used by the people from Steve's hometown of Mandi. I still lacked the language skills to keep up. I knew everyone was talking about the job, but that was about it.

Finally, curiosity got the better of me. I interrupted the family's loud talk. "What are you saying?"

Steve started to explain. "I have been hired as Assistant Conservator of Forests, and my first posting is at Rohru."

This surprised me. I expected his first assignment to be in the capital city of Shimla, where we now lived. There had been rumors that his posting would be in the remote town of Rohru, which was seventy miles from Shimla, but I had ignored them. I had been sure the Chief Conservator would not send us to a remote area. Wasn't Steve the only man in the forest department with a Doctor of Forestry degree? Besides, nobody else had an American wife. At least at Shimla, I had some English-speaking friends and relatives. My heart sank. With this job posting, I would have to start over again in a small town not much bigger than a village.

Steve read my mind and said, "It won't be so bad. We'll stay in the forest rest house.[20] Rohru is not the typical, remote small town. It's famous for trout fishing, and foreign tourists visit during the fishing season."

Before Steve could say anything more, he had to translate what he had just told me so family members could understand. With continual translations, it would be a long time before I found out much. I decided to ask Babu-ji to explain what was being said. As usual, he was sitting quietly at the edge of the group, listening intently to everything. He didn't talk constantly like the rest of the family. When he spoke, he always had something important to say, and everyone listened to him. Hindi was Babu-ji's first language, but he felt equally comfortable speaking and writing in English, which had been required for his law school. Throughout his government career as a judge, most of his court work had been in English.

Babu-ji's dark brown eyes sparkled as he translated for me. He listened attentively to the conversations and explained what was said. He spoke softly, but his voice carried an enthusiasm that I hadn't noticed for a long time. We had never mentioned to Babu-ji that if Steve could

---

[20] A guest house for visiting officials

Job Celebration

not get a job soon, we would need to return to the United States, but I was sure he had sensed our thoughts.

I listened carefully to Babu-ji as he added what he knew about Rohru. He said, "It's more like a village than a town, and it has a small hospital. Most of the officers who work there don't keep their families with them. The officials are on tour a lot, and Rohru schools are like village schools, so families live in their hometowns, where they have better facilities."

As Babu-ji continued to translate, I envisioned a village in a valley with a trout stream running past the rest house, a dispensary-like hospital, and not much more. Yet I began to warm to the idea. Taking care of Raju, our baby son, and managing our home would keep me busy. Also, I was confident that with practice I'd learn Hindi, particularly since not many people there knew English. Already, I spoke short sentences and understood simple conversations when people spoke slowly.

Then Babu-ji added, "You and Raju will stay at Shimla for a couple of months until Madhu is settled at Rohru."

This statement caught me completely off guard. There was no way that I would stay behind. No matter what, I was going with Steve! Usually, when Babu-ji made a family decision, nobody questioned him. This time it would have to be different. I knew that after the celebrations were over, I would need to question his decision that Raju and I stay back at Shimla.

Once the excitement and confusion died down, Steve's mother, Ama-ji, and his sisters went to the kitchen to prepare a celebratory tea. Raju started crying in the bedroom. I went to feed him, and Steve followed. It was our first chance to talk alone about the move. We agreed that although we appreciated the family's hospitality, we really wanted our own home.

I finished nursing Raju and began to change his diaper. This took longer than usual, because Steve kept teasing Raju, trying to get him to smile about the new job. Finally, Raju gave a big smile, and I finished changing him.

When I was done, Steve continued to tell Raju about his job. Seeing the serious expressions on both their faces made me wonder: Maybe Raju did understand that we were about to start on a new adventure. Then I put Raju in his Indian-style crib, which was a wooden frame that had a hanging wooden crib in it that swung like a hammock. I rocked him until he fell asleep. Eventually, there was a knock at the door, and Steve opened it.

Amaj-ji stood in the doorway. She wore a brown *salwar kameez* and a matching *dupatta*. Her clothes were immaculately clean. Not for the first time, I wondered how she kept them so neat and clean when she spent so many long hours in the kitchen cooking over a charcoal fire and a kerosene stove. Ama-ji loved cooking, and there was plenty of it with so many guests. She always had a cheerful look on her face, but now she looked particularly excited.

She said, *"Bahar auo, chai tiar hai."* ("Come out, tea is ready.") She looked at me to see if I understood.

I acted out drinking a cup of tea and said, *"Mai samajh gai."* ("I understand.")

Ama-ji laughed kindly, and we followed her into the living room, which had no windows and only one dim light. The one luxury item in the room was a large shortwave radio, which was playing Indian popular music. The wood floor was bare except for a rug in the center of the room. Today the room had a festive air. A table was set with glasses for tea, empty plates, and a variety of snacks. Ama-ji had prepared my favorite grilled sandwiches stuffed with tomatoes. Also she had made *pakoras*—fried potatoes and spinach in a batter of chickpea flour seasoned with hot peppers, turmeric, salt, coriander, and cumin—which were served with a mint *chutney*, a sweet-and-sour spicy sauce. I noticed two plates of pakoras on the table.

Ama-ji pointed to the smaller plate and said, *"Mirch nahi hai."* ("No hot peppers in these.")

I understood that these were made especially for me and Babu-ji. Both of us liked our food with less spices. In addition to the pakoras and tomato sandwiches, there were jelly sandwiches, cashew nuts, cookies, potato cutlets, and fried liver. All of these had been made at home. The only items from the bazaar were Indian sweets. When I saw so much food, I wondered how we would finish everything.

Two sisters-in-law poured the tea. Another sister-in-law and I passed the snacks. When the serving plates were empty, Ama-ji brought out more freshly fried pakoras and grilled sandwiches. These quickly disappeared, and she refilled the serving plates again. Then, she came and joined us. She was always the last to eat. She never ate until everyone was served and had all they wanted. If someone didn't eat as much food as Ama-ji thought they should, she coaxed them to have more.

I poured tea for Ama-ji, and she had pakoras, chutney, and fried liver. Unlike her husband, she preferred highly seasoned food and ate meat. In many Indian families, when the husbands didn't eat meat, the wives stopped eating meat also. However, despite being a strict vegetarian himself, Babu-ji insisted that Ama-ji continue eating meat, as she had done before marriage. He allowed meat to be cooked in the kitchen, as long as it was kept separate from the vegetarian food. Ama-ji sat cross-legged on the floor, ate her food, drank tea, and joined the conversation. Today she had a lot to talk about, since her son had finally secured the much sought after job.

It was a special celebration. The four months of waiting had bothered all of us, even though we didn't discuss our anxiety openly. Steve and I would not have been able to continue to live in India without employment. Now that Steve had his Himachal forestry job, a new life was starting. Steve was excited about the opportunity to use his forestry education from Duke University, and I looked forward to setting up a home in India. I just had to figure out how to convince Babu-ji that Raju and I should accompany Madhu when he went to Rohru.

8

Move to Rohru

How can we convince the family to allow me to go with Steve when he joins his forestry job at Rohru? After four long months of living with in-laws, I desperately wanted to have my own home. However, both Steve and his parents were worried about how Raju and I would manage in the remote area of Rohru. We began to ask friends and family about the place. The only thing we found out for certain was that Rohru had a great reputation for trout fishing. We were told that we would have no trouble with our fish diet because of the abundance of trout in the Pabbar River, which ran below the town. We wanted to know more. *What food other than fish was available? What was the housing situation? What were the medical facilities?* Our list of questions ran on and on. Whenever we asked them, the answers were always vague.

Knowing so little about the area, Babu-ji stuck to his guns.

Raju at five months old

He said, "Madhu will go alone and see what the place is like. You and Raju can follow after he learns more about Rohru."

But even with the uncertainties, I remained totally against this idea. It made little difference to me how good or bad things were. If Steve could live there, so could I. Besides, we had been married less than a year, and the thought of a few months' separation was upsetting.

Finally, we reached a compromise. About a week before Steve was set to leave, we all agreed that I would stay with them in Shimla for a short time until we knew more about housing and medical aid—essentials for a family with a young baby.

Then, as Steve and I walked on the Shimla Mall Road three days before he was to leave, we met an officer who was the magistrate at Rohru. He answered many of our questions. We were delighted to hear that there was electricity in the town, and the forest rest house, where we were to stay on a temporary basis, was well-furnished. He added, "Food, however, is a big problem. Few vegetables are sold in the market. I grow my own vegetables in a small garden behind my house."

We learned a lot more from him. Meat was available once a month, but only if you were lucky enough to get to town before the meat from a couple of slaughtered goats was sold out. The hospital was staffed with one doctor. When he went on vacation, the hospital was run by a compounder.[21] Before leaving us, the magistrate requested, "Please have dinner with my wife and me when you come to Rohru."

I thought, *I'll be there for that dinner.*

Even with the potential challenges to obtain fresh food, the description of Rohru made me certain that Steve, Raju, and I should go together. The three of us could survive there. I glanced at Steve, and he seemed to read the look of determination on my face. For the first time, he agreed that it would not be risky for the three of us to make the initial trip together. All the way home from the Mall, Steve and I discussed arguments that we could use to convince his family that it was safe for us to make the trip together.

We arrived home and pleaded with Steve's parents, telling them about what we had learned. Finally, Babu-ji agreed. "I think it's all right for the three of you to go together."

Ama-ji added in Hindi, "I will come with you to help you get settled."

This took another weight off our minds. As much as I longed for

---

[21] Similar to a pharmacist, this was a person who mixed ingredients for prescriptions, gave the medicine to hospital patients, and sometimes talked to patients about their ailments and made suggestions for treatments.

independence, I knew I would be glad to have her assistance. Setting up a home in India was different from America. Cooking was my biggest worry. There were no supermarkets for buying whatever food items we needed and no four-burner electric stoves with ovens for cooking our meals.

We had two days to get ready for the move. Everybody began to make shopping lists. I made a few suggestions, but these didn't seem very important to the family. They were going to set up our housekeeping Indian style. Since Steve and I didn't have any money of our own, I felt that we shouldn't push our requests. I knew that after we got our first monthly paycheck of four hundred rupees,[22] we could begin to invest in things that we felt were needed.

I went on the shopping trips and made a few choices. I picked out our everyday dishes and stainless steel cutlery, which we bought at the family's favorite crockery store on Mall Road. When it came to cookware and stoves, we walked down to Middle Bazaar, a narrow, crowded road lined with small, open shops on both sides. I felt the family's judgment was better than mine for these purchases. I knew practically nothing about kerosene stoves and brass cookware. I told them to buy the minimum. The best purchases were a pressure cooker and a small electric hot plate. These seemed to be what we would use for most of our cooking.

In fact, Ama-ji said in Hindi, "The electric hot plate is for you to use, and not the servants. The servants can't be trusted with such costly items. They will use a kerosene stove and a wood fire for cooking."

Finally, the day of departure for Rohru arrived. It was scheduled for early morning. We got up at six, but by the time we packed our luggage and loaded it into the two jeeps and a trailer, it was almost noontime. Steve, Raju, and I were in one jeep. The other jeep had Ama-ji, an uncle, and the eight-year-old son of Steve's boss at Rohru. The boy normally lived in Shimla with his mom, brothers, and a sister, but this was his school vacation, so he was going to visit his dad for a week.

Early that evening, we reached the Rohru Forest Rest House, our temporary home, where we were greeted by a small group of forestry staff and Steve's boss. They served us tea on the rest house verandah. Everyone was talking up a storm, most of it in Hindi. Occasionally Steve's boss, the Divisional Forest Officer, spoke to me in English. As the talk continued, I was eager to get to our room and start unpacking.

---

[22] About thirty-five dollars

Steve's boss told me that all I needed to do was unpack our nightclothes and bedding. Dinner was ready for us.

The first morning at the Rohru Forest Rest House, we got up early. Steve was eager to start his new job, and I was keen to begin setting up our temporary living arrangements. We were staying in set number two of the guest house until a government rental house was available. This set had a large furnished bedroom, a small dressing room, and a good-sized bathroom with a flush toilet. The separate kitchen was about thirty feet behind the rest house. It had a wood and charcoal fireplace, pots and pans, and a sink with running water. Fortunately, we didn't have to share the kitchen. We ate our meals in a common dining room, which had a full set of crockery.

This meant Ama-ji and I didn't need to unpack our dishes and cooking utensils. We did unpack the kerosene stove and pressure cooker, however. With the kitchen away from our rooms, I would leave most of the cooking to the servants, who were employed by the forest department. One was the rest house caretaker, and the others were *peons*, office attendants, who also helped out.

Living in the rest house limited what could be done to set up a household. Ama-ji and Uncle realized this, so they helped take out our necessary belongings and put the rest of our things in a storage room. Once this was done, they went back to Shimla.

For the first time in months, I had some downtime that was all my own. I thought, *We are finally setting up our household, and Steve has begun his first Indian job. I can't wait to see how this new chapter in our life unfolds.*

Bumpy Bus Ride in the Mountains

As much as I enjoyed my new freedom at home, I always welcomed the chance to accompany Steve on his various inspection tours of newly planted nurseries and thick forests in his division. Raju was a good little traveler, whether the trips were by jeep, on horseback, or on foot.

One unforgettable trip, different than the usual inspection tours, occurred when Steve, Raju, and I travelled from Rohru to Shimla in a government jeep. This was Steve's first official work tour to the state capital. After two days of meetings, he had to return to Rohru to mark trees for felling before the first snowfall. I stayed in Shimla with his family because our belongings from the United States were due to arrive. Finally they did, and it was time for Raju and me to return to Rohru.

At seven in the morning, an hour before departure time, our travel group reached the crowded Shimla bus terminal. Our group consisted of me (the twenty-year-old foreign *memsahib*), Raju (my four-month-old, fair-skinned baby boy), Unu and Pnu (my six and eight-year-old Indian nephews, who were coming for a visit), and Nicku (our thirteen-year-old domestic servant, who lived with us). We were accompanied to the bus stand by a see-off group of two sisters-in-law, their husbands, and three drivers. I could see that people were staring at us—again.

We had reserved seats that had been purchased by Tilak Uncle, who worked for the Himachal Road Transport Corporation. *Where was Uncle?* He was supposed to arrange for the loading of our twenty-four pieces of luggage on the Rohru bus. Uncle wasn't anywhere to be found, but there were scores of *Gorkha coolies*, Nepali laborers, hovering around and shouting at us to let them help. They were scantily dressed despite the cold December temperature, and I was tempted to cave in to their pleas and hire some of them.

Finally, Uncle appeared in white pajamas and a long, beige pashmina shawl. He took over, chose four coolies, and directed them to carry the luggage from our three jeeps to a rather dilapidated, dusty gray diesel bus with green lettering and a luggage rack that covered the entire top. The coolies hoisted the larger pieces onto their heads to free their hands for smaller pieces and headed for the bus. One by one, they climbed the ladder on the back of the bus and loaded twenty-four pieces of luggage on the roof. I was afraid that they were going to drop some of the bigger and unwieldy pieces of our belongings from America. The box with the portable typewriter went up easily, but our record player almost didn't make it up the ladder. It had taken six months by ship and road for these personal belongings to reach us from Durham, North Carolina. I didn't want any mishaps now.

After our luggage was loaded, we waited in the jeeps for the driver and conductor. When they arrived, passengers rushed in a disorderly manner to board the bus. Most of the travelers were men, but there were a couple of women with their families. I watched the commotion from my brother-in-law's jeep, while I finished breastfeeding Raju. Then, escorted by family members, we made our way to the bus. I felt a gust of chilly wind as my nephews, our servant, baby Raju, and I boarded the bus for our seventy-mile journey, which was supposed to take nine hours. Before sitting down, I checked to make sure our home-cooked food, boiled water, shawls, blankets, and the long-awaited diapers from America were under our front seats.

A half-hour late, the bus started off with a loud, roaring sound. Our see-off relatives said *"Namaste"* and waved as the bus chugged out of the terminal behind another slow-moving vehicle. I felt anxious. It was my first Indian road trip on my own, and I was the only adult in our group. To keep from worrying, I thought back to my busy life with Steve when we were students at Duke University. But my daydreaming quickly ended as the deep ruts in the road jarred me back to reality.

It was chilly in the unheated bus, and we wrapped our shawls around us. The windows remained open for passengers to stick their heads out and vomit when they felt sick. Motion sickness was common on these winding, bumpy, dusty mountain roads. Fortunately, none of us had this problem. I sat with Raju in my lap next to Unu, who loved to use his convent-school English with me. Pnu sat behind us with our servant, Nicku. Both talked nonstop in Hindi. I hardly understood a word of what they said.

We were travelling downhill on a narrow, curvy road and often met a truck loaded with potatoes as we rounded a curve. When we came face to face with another vehicle, we had to back up so the approaching vehicle could get by us. After three hours, we pulled into a muddy, open area that seemed like the middle of nowhere. Then I noticed a small, village-style wooden building off to the side. Passengers started to push and shove to get out.

I asked Unu, "What's happening?"

He said, "Auntie, we are at a *chai dhaba*, tea stall, where we can have tea and something to eat."

I didn't plan to eat or drink anything at the tea stall. My sister-in-law Anjana, Unu and Pnu's mom, had packed enough food and boiled water to last three days. I wanted to go to the bathroom but changed my mind when I heard there were no public restrooms. My nephews and Nicku had no problem going in the woods. The abrupt stop and loud talk of passengers leaving the bus woke Raju up, so I nursed him as I waited for the boys to return from the woods.

After a while, the passengers came back to the bus, picked up their belongings, and returned to the tea stall. Unu, Pnu, and Nicku rushed to the bus.

Clearly excited and nervous, Unu explained, "Auntie, Auntie! There's something wrong with the bus, and they're trying to fix it."

I tried to remain calm in front of my nephews, even though the idea of not being able to reach Rohru unnerved me. I told the boys, "Let's just stay on the bus till they get it fixed."

Unu said that he was hungry, so I took out some *kachoris*—thick, Indian bread stuffed with lentils—and we each had a kachori along with our boiled water. We looked out the window, but nothing seemed to be happening. Most of the passengers were inside the dhaba, drinking hot tea and sitting near a wood fire. The driver was walking around smoking a *beedhi*, a brown, hand-rolled cigarette. The conductor kept coming out from under the bus to tell the driver something.

Finally, the conductor climbed into the bus and informed us that we needed to get off. He said, "Big problem!" Then he added in Hindi that the axle was broken, and he couldn't fix it. Since there were no phones in the dhaba or in the village, we had to wait for another vehicle to relay a message to the bus company at Shimla saying that they needed to send a bus with spare parts and a mechanic to fix our broken-down bus. This rescue vehicle would take us to Rohru.

I asked the boys to tell the conductor that I didn't plan to get off. I desperately wanted to stay on the bus until the rescue vehicle arrived. I needed to keep an eye on our precious luggage, which included wedding gifts ranging from Lenox China to an electric fry pan.

The conductor sensed I was not about to budge. He left, went over to the driver, and talked with him. It started to get dark and uncomfortably cold. I told the boys to open one of our bags under the seats, and we looked for blankets. The conductor and driver got on the bus and talked with my nephews in Hindi. The boys explained to me that we were going to spend the night in this tiny village, and that we had to go into the dhaba for the night. There was one room for sleeping, and they were giving it to us. Probably, we were getting the room because they knew that Uncle was our relative, and they wanted to please their boss. The driver, half in broken English and half in Hindi, said that most of the passengers would be getting back on the bus to sleep, and it was safer and warmer inside the tea stall. After more arguing, I reluctantly agreed. The conductor got our bedroll off the roof of the bus and carried it into the dhaba.

We followed him into the smoke-filled tea stall and were escorted into our room. It had one, small kerosene lantern near a pile of bulging burlap bags of rice, wheat flour, and potatoes. In this tiny room there was one bed, and it had jute strings woven together in a spring-like arrangement. Nicku put my mattress and quilt on the bed, and the dhaba owner brought in a thin, cotton-filled mattress and a quilt for the boys. Raju and I slept on the bed, while the boys were on the floor surrounded by stacks of burlap bags. Once it got dark, Unu took me outside to go to the bathroom in the woods. Unu and I returned, and we settled in for the night. I tried to sleep. It was scary with the lantern off and all kinds of suspicious sounds. I was pretty sure the pitter-patter that sounded like raindrops was mice running around. I felt bad for the poor boys on the floor. Thank goodness they were sound sleepers.

Finally, it was morning, and we all went outside. The driver and conductor greeted us and informed us in Hindi, "A rescue bus should be here in an hour. Please eat something in the dhaba before we resume our journey."

I wouldn't touch the tea stall food and wanted to eat more of our packed food, which needed to be warmed. I was afraid to hand it over to the tea stall owner for warming, because I questioned the cleanliness of everything I had seen so far. My nephews and Nicku wanted to try *aloo ka parantha*, lightly fried bread made from wheat flour and stuffed with potatoes. The owner was roasting the paranthas on a *tawa*, griddle. The boys begged me to let them have the bread, which was being cooked over a wood fire. I reluctantly agreed.

Raju had his breast milk and was in my arms most of the time because I didn't feel comfortable putting him on the bus seat. The only time I put Raju down was when I changed his diapers. I was glad to have the American plastic pants and cloth diapers, which were much more absorbent than Indian diapers and kept me from having to change him too often. I was afraid that I'd run out of clean diapers.

Suddenly, we heard a bus pull into the muddy yard beside the dhaba, and everyone rushed outside. The bus drove up beside ours. Passengers climbed onto the rooftops and handed each piece of luggage from the roof of the disabled bus to the passengers on the roof of the second vehicle. They struggled with the heavier pieces but were successful. I was relieved when my luggage made the transfer safely.

Then we all got on the rescue bus and started the uphill climb to Karthapathar, which was almost 8,000 feet (2,438 meters) above sea level. We were lucky that we had spent the night at about 3,000 feet (914 meters), where the cold was tolerable. The ruts in the road got worse, and sometimes it felt like we'd roll over when the tires on one side of the bus were in a deep rut, and the tires on the other side were on the flat, muddy road. Most of the trip, the road was unpaved.

We made a few quick stops and reached Rohru at three in the afternoon. The bus stopped at the forest rest house, our temporary home. There was a forest guard and a *chaukidar* (caretaker) waiting for us on the road below the rest house. The forest guard helped us off the bus and unloaded our bags from inside the bus. He asked, "Is there any luggage on the roof?"

The boys cried out, "Oh yes, twenty-four pieces!" As I walked around to the back of the bus and watched the forestry staff climb up to the roof, Steve came around from the other side. He lovingly took Raju from my arms, kissed him, and gave me a smile of relief.

15

Following the Rivers and Setting up a Home

While Steve's nephews spent their three-month winter school break with us, he was assigned to *ghal duty*. This meant that he had to accompany the timber that was being floated down the river to where it would be auctioned off. The timber from the forest was floated down a narrow mountain stream to the roadside near Sawra and then launched into the Pabbar River. Steve was to follow along

Sleepers on the way to the timber auction

the Pabbar and Tons rivers with his forestry staff to make sure that the lumber reached Dehradun safely. Since he would be away for a long time, we decided that the boys and I would accompany him.

We left Rohru in Steve's government jeep. On the third day of the trip in early February we switched to horseback riding and hiking. Our luggage was loaded onto four mules. Sometimes we stayed in rest houses, and other times we camped out. Raju was least of all challenged by this trip. He had his breast milk, his mom to bathe him, his dad to talk to him, and his cousins to play with. When we hiked, he was carried by a forestry staff person.

During our trip, I bathed Raju in a plastic wash basin while I sat on an Indian-style bed, which had a platform made of woven jute strings attached to a wooden frame and four wooden legs. After his bath, I dressed him in a brown hand-knit sweater and a green outfit made by our tailor.

One highlight of the trip occurred when the boys rode in the river on an inflated buffalo skin. It was a sunny day, and we were about 1,500 feet above sea level so the weather was quite pleasant. Unu, Pnu, and Raju were helped onto the inflated buffalo skin by a forest guard, who then sat with them and paddled the

Steve with Raju sitting on a goat

Steve and Raju at the edge of a stream on ghal duty

Elma sitting on a bed before bathing Raju

Elma, Unu, Pnu, Raju, and horse handler

Riding on the inflated buffalo

buffalo skin like a boat. He kept the buffalo boat close to the shore, and the boys called out, "Look at us!" I swam along beside them. Steve watched from the shore, cheering us along, as we tried to keep away from the floating timber. I was amazed at all the exciting adventures I was having in our new life together.

Late spring of 1963, I was finally able to be a real homemaker when we were transferred six miles from Rohru to Sawra. Steve had been given a new job assignment, and we were allotted a two-story government accommodation with a small undeveloped yard surrounding the house.

Having a kitchen inside the rental house made it much easier for me to get involved in the cooking. The kitchen was very basic, with cement floors and counters. There were a few wooden cabinets and a sink with a cement wash basin. There was a hearth for cooking over a wood fire and a separate one for charcoal. The kitchen had running cold water. I started unpacking our kitchen supplies and quickly took out our kerosene stove and electric hot plate. Next, I unpacked the cooking utensils we had bought at Shimla. I placed the brass cooking pots and pans on an open shelf along with the pressure cooker and was ready to start my first cooking experience by making tea.

Steve and I had tea together, and I couldn't stop talking about our first real kitchen. I told him that I had unpacked many of our Indian kitchen utensils and planned to go through the things we had brought from America, which were still unpacked. Steve, who is usually not much of a talker, added a lot of suggestions about where his favorite items should be placed. I hadn't opened it yet, but he wanted our record player in the living room.

The next day I opened the boxes we had packed a long time ago in North Carolina. The first box I opened had a heavy black transformer for changing 220 volts to 110. It was going to be useful. Next, I opened a box with an electric fry pan, a blender, and a coffee pot. I tried plugging the transformer into the wall socket, but it didn't fit. Luckily I had a spare Indian plug, and our servant helped by using it to replace the American plug. Next, I opened a wooden box with our three speed record player. I plugged it in the transformer and turned it on. It worked pretty well, except that the speed for the records was off a little bit.

Then, I carefully unpacked our Lenox China and Pyrex bowls. Luckily, nothing was broken. This was followed by our stainless steel cutlery set. All of these were wedding or shower gifts from America.

I did most of the unpacking as Raju watched me or sat on the floor playing with measuring spoons and cups. Our servant Nicku helped with entertaining Raju. We paid Nicku fifty rupees[23] a month as well as giving him free room and board. We also bought all his clothes and anything else he needed. In addition, a woman came three times a week to wash clothes. She did this in our downstairs bathroom while sitting on a small wooden platform. She soaked the clothes in a bucket of hot water. Then she checked to see if they needed hand scrubbing or being beaten with a flat piece of wood about eighteen inches long, three inches wide, and two inches thick. Next she rinsed the clothes in cold water. We also employed a part-time sweeper, who cleaned the bathrooms. I was fine with all this help. When I was a youngster in New Jersey, my grandparents had live-in help. Their home was around the corner from ours.

When Raju started crawling around to places he shouldn't be, I put him in his folding wooden playpen, which had been made by a carpenter in Shimla's Lakhar Bazaar, the shopping area that specialized in making and selling wooden toys and other wooden pieces. I had brought roller wheels from the United States, and I gave these to

---

[23] Five dollars

the carpenter for the four legs and showed him pictures to use while crafting the playpen. He did an excellent job, especially since he'd never seen one.[24] Ama-ji had never liked to see Raju in the playpen, but I thought it was an excellent way for me to get things done while I was sure he was safe.

In fact, it had turned out that Ama-ji and I had different views on many different aspects of child rearing. For instance, she loved putting *kajal*, black eyeliner, around Raju's eyes, which was supposed to help his vision. I didn't like the looks of the black lines around his blue eyes and thought the black clashed with his fair skin and golden brown hair. During our time at Shimla, Ama-ji also bathed Raju each day. For this process, she always sat on the floor, put her feet in the wash basin, added warm water, and then placed Raju on her crossed legs and feet. Now her hands were free to soap and wash him. After his bath, my mother-in-law oiled and massaged him daily for at least fifteen minutes. I desperately wanted to bathe Raju myself in the plastic basin, while holding him with one hand and washing with the other—no feet in the basin. However, as long as we lived in Shimla, I never had a chance to bathe him.

Another sore point with Ama-ji stemmed from the fact that Raju refused to take a bottle. This meant I could hardly ever leave him with my mother-in-law. When I did leave him for a short period, Ama-ji complained, *"Raju bahut roya doodh ke liya."* ("Raju cried a lot for milk.") She added that I shouldn't leave him so long, and she felt cruel not being able to satisfy him. I thought that he was fine without milk for two hours.

The new freedom I felt in Rohru and Sawra was refreshing. I bathed Raju according to my style, stopped using the *kajal*, lightly oiled him before his bath with mustard oil, and massaged him for a few minutes, but nothing as extensive as Ama-ji did.

After unpacking all the boxes and putting things in convenient places, I decided to try baking a cake in the electric fry pan, since we didn't have an Indian oven. I took out my red-and-white Betty Crocker cookbook and found a made-from-scratch cake recipe. Luckily, I had bought baking powder during my last visit to Shimla. After checking that I had all the ingredients, I started mixing them in one of my Pyrex bowls, using my electric egg beater. Once the batter was

---

[24] I never saw a playpen in any of the places we stayed in India. Once, a passerby saw Raju in his playpen on our porch and remarked, "Why do you keep your child in an animal cage?"

ready, I poured it into the preheated electric fry pan and waited for the suggested thirty-five minutes. Raju watched me throughout the process. I opened the lid, touched the top of the cake, which sprang back, and then poked a toothpick in it, which came out clean. Raju saw me do it and pointed at the cake, indicating he wanted it. He tried a small piece, and he gestured for more.

Another day while Raju was in his playpen, he was upset and cried a lot. At first I couldn't figure out what the problem was. I noticed his favorite yellow blanket drying on the porch and brought it in. The minute I gave him the yellow blanket, he grabbed it, held it against his cheeks, and stopped crying. After that, I cut the blanket into two pieces, hemmed the raw edges, and gave him half a blanket at a time. When I washed one piece, he had the other half to keep him happy. The yellow blanket problem was solved.

After six months Steve was promoted to Divisional Forest Officer (D.F.O.) and was transferred back to Rohru. At this time, the D.F.O.'s government residence was ready. This meant we moved our belongings from a two-bedroom house to a much larger, three-bedroom house. Again I spent my days unpacking and putting things away. I felt like an expert by now.

Once the unpacking was done, I started to work in a large garden area off to one side of the house. The previous D.F.O.'s gardener had only planted seeds in one small plot. The plants looked like radish plants.

I surveyed the area and made plans for how to set up the garden. I was able to get some seeds in the Rohru bazaar but not as many varieties as I wanted. I planned to get more seeds the next time we visited Shimla. Vegetable gardening was a necessity. The local market had only potatoes, onions, and sometimes dried up radishes and turnips.

Whenever the weather was good, I spent hours in the garden, preparing plots, planting seeds, watering plants, and weeding. Usually, Raju was with me while I worked. He had a few gardening tools of his own and copied whatever I was doing. At the end of two growing seasons, I had fifteen different varieties of vegetables.

Pnu, Raju, and Unu in Auckland House school uniforms

Fishing in Himachal Pradesh

Spring arrived and the trout fishing season opened. We were fortunate to live close to the Pabbar River, which originated high in the Himalayas and ran below the town of Rohru. This river was one of the first places where trout were introduced in India. The trout were brought from England by boat in the 1930s and stocked in the Pabbar River. The fish fared well since the climate and environment were similar to their habitat in England. The most popular fishing spots on the Pabbar were along a twelve-mile stretch near the small town of Rohru.

Steve and I loved fishing. When it was just the two of us fishing, we were accompanied by a forest guard and a few other forestry staff. Our son, Raju, usually came along with us and was carried and entertained by Gia Lal, who was an office attendant but also worked in our home and went with us on Steve's different work assignments. He and Raju got along well.

Steve was new to the sport. I had fished for bass, perch, and sunfish while growing up in America, but I had never fished for trout. Both of us learned the sport quickly. I enjoyed wading into the water while fishing. Steve stayed on the riverbanks. He was afraid of the water, because he couldn't swim. A forest guard usually went into the water for him, if his lure got stuck on a rock.

We always bought fishing licenses, even though a staff member remarked, "You're an officer. You can fish for free." We believed that the rules regarding licenses, number of fish, and size were for everyone.

Fishing in Himachal Pradesh

Many local residents and villagers were discouraged from fishing because of the expensive licensing fees. It cost five rupees[25] per day. With a one-day license, a fisherman was allowed to keep six fish, which were required to be nine inches or longer in length. That wasn't enough to feed a villager's large family. Therefore, not many villagers could afford a license. Still, there were a few with the fishing bug, and they often spent a month's earnings on licenses.

Steve holding a trout he caught

The most common equipment for the local fishermen was a simple, Indian bamboo pole and steel reel. Usually, they had a couple of foreign-made lures and spinners. Some locals were professional in their handling of the crudest bamboo rods. They appeared more graceful than the visiting fishermen with their foreign rods and reels. Besides looking so nimble, they often caught more than the city visitors.

Not all the locals were experienced sportsmen with standard equipment. There were times when an amateur fisherman tried his luck and caught a trout with simple, homemade tackle. One time, I watched an amateur use a lure and some string, which he tied onto a stick. With this stick for a fishing pole and no reel, he made two awkward casts. On his second cast, I was amazed to see him hook and catch a five-inch trout.

Another time, I watched an eight-year-old boy with even simpler gear. The young boy attached a live fly to a long piece of string and dangled it in the water. Within a short time, he caught a small trout, much to the surprise of his father, who didn't catch anything all day.

---

[25] Fifty cents

Most of the out-of-town fishermen stayed at the forest rest house during their fishing trips. One of the most spectacular fishing parties to visit was a Maharajah from Punjab and his staff of thirty. He was called a Maharajah because his ancestors had been Maharajahs when the British governed much of India. He no longer ruled, but he had a substantial inheritance from the time his ancestors were in command. When the Maharajah came to fish, he liked to have the same luxurious comforts he enjoyed at home. He brought a four-piece band, a large cooking staff, a private secretary, jeep drivers, sweepers, and personal servants. There was even staff to take care of the staff. But the Maharajah didn't bring his friends from his home state of Punjab. If he wanted company, he invited the local fishing enthusiasts to join him. He quickly made friends with government officials, residents of the town, and nearby villagers. Steve and I fished and partied with him.

Enthusiastic young fishermen were encouraged by the Maharajah, and he was generous with his expensive equipment from Europe and America. If a local person needed fishing lure, he gave him a couple pieces. After fishing during the day, his favorite pastimes were drinking, eating, and playing bridge into the wee hours of the night. Steve often joined him for his bridge games and parties. No matter how late the Maharajah played bridge or how much he drank, he was almost always out on the stream by six in the morning.

One morning there was an exception. The Maharajah left the rest house early, but along the way to his favorite fishing spot, he met a villager in need of medical aid, so he drove the man to the Rohru Government Hospital. With his kindness, warm personality, large staff, and fancy equipment, all of the locals who met the Maharajah admired him greatly. Between visits, everyone hoped he would return soon.

In contrast to the extravagant Maharajah and his many staff members was a fisherman who came from Chandigarh, Mr. Oelwein. This German fisherman brought only a jeep driver and a personal servant. Mr. Oelwein was an avid fisherman. He left Chandigarh at three in the morning and drove straight through to Rohru in ten grueling hours. Then he showered, ate lunch, and took a short nap. After his nap, Mr. Oelwein hiked down to the river. On his first afternoon fishing, he caught the biggest trout of the season. I was lucky enough to be with him. The six-and-a-half pound trout fought for twenty minutes after it was hooked. Wow! What a struggle!

Besides catching large trout, he always caught the daily limit of six fish per fishing license. Instead of eating all the fish he caught, he put them on ice in his portable ice chest. Local residents, who had never seen an ice chest, nicknamed Mr. Oelwein, *"Bahar ki admi frig ke sath."* ("Foreigner with a refrigerator.") The fish he caught at Rohru were taken in the ice chest to Chandigarh and put in his imported, full-size refrigerator. He enjoyed the refrigerated fish for the next month at Chandigarh, where trout fish were a delicacy. Mr. Oelwein's visits usually lasted only a day or two, but he packed in the maximum fishing time and maximum number of fish during his short stays.

Every year more and more fishermen discovered the thrill of trout fishing at Rohru. Some learned about this special fishing spot from a brochure put out by the Himachal Forest Department, but the best advertisement was word of mouth from fishermen like the Maharajah, Mr. Oelwein, and other regulars. They described the small town tucked away in the Pabbar Valley as a fisherman's paradise. They admitted it was tough to reach Rohru, but they also insisted that it was well worth the effort. If there had been a fisherman's map, Rohru would have been on it in bold letters.

12

A Trip to Mandi and a Forest Inspection Tour

Shortly before Raju turned a year old, we made a trip to Mandi. It was Raju's and my first visit to Madhu's hometown. Naturally, we stayed at the ancestral home of my in-laws which was near the shops in the town.

View of Mandi town from a distance

A Trip to Mandi and a Forest Inspection Tour

We had a small bedroom on the first floor of the house. The windows on two walls of the room were very high because they looked out on the narrow streets just below them. At night we could hear pedestrians as they walked on the street. Our bedroom was next to a living room which we had to cross to get to the small bathroom, which had a flush toilet and an area for bucket showers. Babu-ji, Ama-ji, Buri Mata-ji, and Madhu's sister Vidya lived on the second floor of the house. They had their own bathroom, and there was one kitchen in the house.

Mandi town close up

We had come to Mandi because a big celebration was planned for Raju's first birthday. On his birthday, he wore a pink, Indian outfit made by a local tailor and decorated with silver-like ribbons. At his birthday party, the older children received

Raju's first birthday party at Mandi

whistle noisemakers, which they were constantly blowing. At first the squeaky whistling sounds scared Raju, but he got used to them. We gave him one of the noise makers. He tried blowing it but couldn't make any sounds, so he waved it around.

As part of the celebration, we were served snacks of *pakora* (deep-fried vegetables in a chick pea batter), *aloo tikki* (fried potato cake), and *burfi* (an Indian sweet). The children continued playing for a couple of hours while the adults talked. The last event was a dinner of rice, lentils, vegetables, and *kheer* (rice pudding).

After our two-week vacation at Mandi, we returned to Rohru. It

Raju with cousins at Mandi

was a busy work time for Madhu. As soon as he got back, he had to make an inspection tour of a dense forest. Raju and I accompanied him on this tour, which was mainly a hiking trip. We loved trips where we hiked and rode horseback. We were accompanied by uniformed, forestry staff, which included officers, rangers, guards, *peons* (office workers), and men who cared for the horses and mules. At first, Raju rode with me on my small horse. He patted the horse and asked to go faster. On the steep, rocky paths, Raju was carried by our attendant, Gia Lal. They talked with each other in Hindi.

When we reached the interior rest house, a *chaukidar* (caretaker) and local forestry staff greeted us. Tea was immediately served. Raju didn't drink tea, but he certainly enjoyed the biscuits, pakoras, and fried potatoes. After our tea, Madhu went for a short inspection trip. Raju and I stayed back at the rest house. I sat in the sunny front yard and watched Raju and Gia Lal play a game of catch. I was fine when he was with forestry staff but only under my watchful eye. If servants, drivers, and other staff wanted to take him to the kitchen or their quarters, I never allowed it. I was quite protective.

The sun set, and we went into the rest house, which was quite cool. We were at 8,000 feet above sea level. Madhu returned and the chaukidar lit a fire in the large stone fireplace. Madhu and his assistant sat by the fire, discussed politics, and had drinks. I read to Raju from a Dr. Seuss book until a sumptuous dinner was served, which included wild chicken curry. A forest guard had shot the chicken in a nearby forest especially for our dinner. The rest of the trip continued in a similar pattern.

13

Ice Skating at Shimla

The record "Cindy Oh Cindy" played over the loudspeaker. I stood at the edge of the rink, watching the skaters glide by in time to the music. It was January of 1965. The cold Shimla air penetrated my red ski sweater and plaid, woolen slacks. I shivered. Then I quickly skated onto the ice and joined the crowd of skaters, who were moving in a clockwise direction. The smooth ice reminded me of a skating rink in Michigan, even though most of the skaters here were Indians.

Halfway around the rink, I saw a group of pre-teen boys playing ice hockey. Their game was at the far end beyond the circling skaters. One team wore red shirts and the other green. As I skated past them, an enthusiastic player on the red team stick-handled the puck out of bounds. His opponent followed closely behind him. The player in the red shirt had his head down and was concentrating on the puck as he headed straight towards me.

Suddenly a third player saw my predicament and shouted, "Look out for the foreigner!" The two players skating towards me looked up and skated around me, narrowly missing a head-on collision.

This was my third winter in India, but it was my first visit to Shimla during the ice skating season. Tonight I came for ice skating by myself because Madhu had to work late at the forest department head office. He planned to meet me at the rink after work. I had left Raju, now two years old, at Madhu's sister's home, where we were staying. Raju loved playing with his cousins and was well-cared for by family members. It was special to be on my own. I didn't like leaving Raju alone with our servant but felt comfortable leaving him with my sister-in-law Anjana.

The open air rink was approximately the size of a United States National Hockey League arena. A high fence of unpainted wooden boards surrounded the skating area. To the right of the narrow entranceway were bleachers, where Shimla residents and tourists sat and watched the ice skaters. To the left of the entrance were wooden park benches, where the skaters changed from their street shoes to ice skates. There were two sections. One was marked *Ladies* and the other *Men*. Many skaters disregarded the signs and didn't worry about sitting and changing into skates according to gender.

People warmed their hands and feet as they sat near the *angithis* (small, square, open iron containers filled with burning charcoal). The ice for the rink was made by flooding the rink in the early morning, when it was cold enough for the water to freeze. If the temperature wasn't cold enough, there wasn't any skating. During the summer, the rink was converted into tennis courts.

The music changed to "The Blue Danube Waltz." Couples danced around the rink. One couple waltzed so gracefully that I imagined judges in a competition giving them high scores for their difficult twists and turns. The woman wore tan tights, a matching sweater, and a patchwork-quilted, skating skirt. Her coal-black hair was pulled back into a long ponytail tied with a tan ribbon and pompons. The pompons swung from side to side as her partner whirled her around the rink. Their long strides matched exactly. They never missed a beat. I knew the woman skater but not her partner. He had on slacks and a green, V-neck, woolen sweater. Under the sweater, he wore a white dress shirt unbuttoned at the collar. I'm sure that he came straight from an office, where men dressed in business suits and ties.

After the record ended, I went over to the couple, introduced myself, and complimented them. "I wish I could skate like both of you."

The man introduced himself as Mr. Sharma and said, "It's easy. Let's try a couple of turns to see how well you do."

I told him, "I know how to skate and dance, but I've never tried dancing on ice."

He seemed surprised, and remarked, "I thought American skaters were good ice dancers."

"You be the judge."

We started to waltz. I should say that my partner started to waltz. I couldn't follow his steps. Mr. Sharma realized that I didn't know what

I was doing. We stopped skating. He showed me some fundamental waltz steps. I watched and then tried them. Mr. Sharma was a patient teacher, but I had a lot to learn. During the lesson, I found out that he was a clerical worker for the Himachal government and often came to skate after work. Then he introduced me to some women who were working on their waltz steps, and we practiced together. They were much better than I was but were willing to help me. As soon as Mr. Sharma saw that I felt comfortable with his Indian students, he and his partner skated off.

After twenty minutes of practice, one of the women suggested, "Let's have coffee in the restaurant."

We all agreed. Still wearing our skates, we climbed up the wooden steps to the restaurant and found an empty table where we could watch the skaters. The restaurant had a tin roof, and the side that faced the skating rink was completely open. As soon as we sat down, a waiter dressed in a white uniform and white turban came to take our order.

Now that we weren't skating, we felt the icy-cold winter weather and looked forward to our hot coffee. We introduced ourselves. On my left was Mrs. Singh, who I guessed was about thirty. She was dressed in a bright maroon *salwar kameez*. The ends of her *dupatta* were tied in a knot halfway down her back so they wouldn't interfere with her skating. The second woman, Mrs. Malhotra, had on black slacks and a sky-blue, hand-knit sweater. Her black hair was pulled back from her face and twisted into an attractive bun. She wore western slacks like many of the other female skaters. Slacks were one of the few western clothes that Indian women wore. It was considered indecent for women to have bare legs, so skirts were unacceptable. My Indian family members didn't mind me wearing slacks but didn't like me wearing skirts and dresses. They were always giving me Indian clothes in hopes that I would stop wearing my American clothes.

Mrs. Malhotra and Mrs. Singh spoke fluent English, so I didn't have to worry about talking in broken Hindi sentences. First, we chatted about skating and how much we loved the activity. Then the conversation turned to talk about our families. All of us had children at home. Mrs. Singh's six-year-old son was with her servant, and Mrs. Malhotra's two children were being cared for by their *dadi*, paternal grandmother.

Mrs. Singh asked, "Who cares for children in America?"

I explained about babysitters and added, "Most married couples don't live with their in-laws or parents. If grandparents live close by, they might do some babysitting, but they aren't always available."

Then I told them about my family. When I was a young girl in New Jersey, my maternal grandparents lived around the block. I spent a lot of time with them. At age ten my family moved to Michigan, and both sets of grandparents remained in New Jersey. This surprised the women. It was hard for them to believe that the different generations in American families didn't live in the same household. Here in India, they were used to having in-laws living with them most of their married life.

I changed the topic to talk about Shimla. Mrs. Singh mentioned that the year-round population of the town was in the thirty thousands. However, during the summer tourist season, this figure often tripled. The hotels were always filled, and residents of Shimla had many guests.

Mrs. Singh said, "In summer I have more guests than beds in my home. When this happens, I adopt a system called *dunghard*, a sleeping arrangement in which my living room floor is covered with thin cotton mattresses, sheets, and blankets to accommodate the extra guests at night."

Mrs. Malhotra added, "Shimla is popular because of the year-round cool weather, old buildings, sightseeing, restaurants, and shopping. Visitors from the plains come here to escape the hot weather and experience winter snow."

As we were talking, I felt a tap on my shoulder. I checked to see who was behind me. Madhu said, "Hi, honey. Are you ready to go home?"

I looked at my watch. It was almost time for the rink to close. I introduced Madhu to Mrs. Malhotra and Mrs. Singh. They excused themselves and went back for a couple more rounds on the ice.

I started to tell Madhu about my evening. Halfway through the description, he interrupted me to say, "I haven't seen you so enthusiastic for a long time. I'll have to come with you tomorrow."

I said, "Yes, you'll love it here where people from different backgrounds interact."

We left the rink and headed home. During the long walk home, I couldn't stop talking about how much fun I had skating.

14

The Unexpected

Raju had received a green tricycle for his first birthday, and riding was now his favorite pastime. At first, Madhu or I pushed him around while he sat on the bike. It took him almost a year before he was able to pedal on his own. He particularly loved riding on our upstairs deck. The deck was basically a large, open porch with a smooth cement floor that made the pedaling easy. As Raju circled the porch, we heard the "toot-toot" of his horn.

Sometimes he rode the cycle in our front yard. The stony dirt paths made riding a challenge. One day he rode his bike to the vegetable garden at the side of our house,

Raju on his tricycle

where I was weeding a tomato plot. Sometimes he pushed his cycle on the garden's grassy pathways, and other times he was able to ride it.

When he rode by me, he shouted in Hindi. "Mom, look at me!" I answered in English. "Great job, keep moving!"

Raju also loved his wooden toys, which came from Lakhar Bazaar. His favorite was a wooden rocking horse. He also liked a set of wooden blocks. He piled the blocks on top of each other until they toppled over. We had a contest where each of us added one block at a time to our structures. If my building toppled first, Raju got excited and shouted, "Mommy, I won, I won!"

One afternoon, he took out his top and asked me to spin it. I showed him how to do it. After a couple of tries, he made the top do a wobbly spin. Madhu and I were so proud of each of his milestones.

Raju and Elma on his rocking horse

It was a sunny March day. Raju was riding his green tricycle on our upstairs porch. Madhu and I sat in wooden chairs and lovingly watched Raju in his green, corduroy jacket. He circled the deck and waved each time he passed us. I remembered that he was due for an antibiotic pill, which he had been

Raju sitting on his rocking horse with his Dad on Rohru porch

The Unexpected

taking for a flu-like fever that he had almost recovered from. I went into the house, cut the pill in half, and filled a glass with water. I returned to the porch and called Raju for his medicine. He came, and I gave him the pill. When he tried to swallow the half-pill, it got caught in his throat. He started to choke, and immediately I thumped his back, trying to dislodge the pill. When he kept choking, we rushed to the local hospital. We started on foot, and then our jeep driven by our driver caught up and rushed us to the hospital. We got there in record time, but Raju was no longer conscious.

On arrival, Raju was immediately looked at by a doctor in a makeshift emergency room. Within a few minutes the doctor came out of the room and said, "I'm sorry, but I couldn't save him. Your son Raju was dead on arrival."

Both Madhu and I collapsed in grief. Neither of us could speak. I couldn't believe the doctor's words. I felt numb. *How could our cherished, blue-eyed son be gone?*

The doctor said that we should go home and wait for the cremation next morning. Once it was clear that nothing could be done to save Raju, we returned home in the jeep. Arriving home was like a nightmare. *What had I done wrong when I gave Raju his medicine?* I was angry and upset with myself.

Madhu and I sat quietly in our living room for a while, unable to talk or cry. Our servant offered us tea, but we said *no*. After a short time, Madhu and I went upstairs. We went directly to our bedroom, avoiding Raju's bedroom and the sun porch. Later our servant came upstairs and asked if we wanted something to eat. We both said *no* and the servant left. Madhu and I looked at each other but couldn't say anything. I couldn't even cry.

The next morning Raju was cremated along the rocky riverside, where a brief service was performed. Madhu and I shed a few tears as we watched the service. We walked back to our home, trying to make sense of what happened. *How could our only child be taken away from us at such an early age?* Back at the house many friends came to pay their condolences. We sat in our living room on a thin carpet that covered the cold cement floor. As people entered, they sat cross-legged on the floor. Little was said at first. Then a few people spoke softly, expressing their shock and sorrow at our untimely loss.

A local farmer sat near us. He tried to console us with a story in Hindi: "When God chooses people to bring into his kingdom, he is like a visitor in an apple orchard. He searches the orchard and then picks out the best apple he can find. Your son, Raju, was the best child God could find, so he chose him for his kingdom. He's in a good place."

The mourning period with visitors coming to our house for a couple of hours each day lasted two weeks. Madhu and I hardly said a word; we simply listened as friends tried to console us. At that time, it seemed that their presence and words did little to help us with our overwhelming grief. Two weeks back, our only child, Raju, was full of life, and now he was gone forever. *How could we exist without him? It wasn't fair. Children were supposed to go after their parents.*

In the evenings when Madhu and I were alone, I tried to talk with him about our loss. He said, "Talk won't help, I don't want to talk about what happened."

I cancelled a trip I had planned to visit my parents in the United States. I knew I couldn't leave Madhu alone at this time.

When the mourning period at Rohru was over, we left for Madhu's home town to be with his parents. At Mandi we went through the customary mourning rituals again, with friends and relatives visiting our family home. We sat on the maroon cement floor of the verandah, which was covered with rugs for this occasion. Everyone sat on the floor with us. There was little talking and much crying. Being with family and friends helped a little with our loss.

After our short visit to Mandi, we returned to Rohru. Madhu went back to work, and I tried to keep busy at home, but it was hard. It seemed like there was nothing for me to do without Raju to care for. I spent some time in my garden but missed Raju riding his bicycle as I worked. I did some housework, but most of it was done by servants. Reading was one way I escaped the loneliness. Still, I felt empty as soon as I put my book down. Friends visited and said time was the best healer. So far, I didn't feel this healing and wondered when—or even if—I would ever feel better.

Madhu continued to be quiet about missing Raju. I wanted to talk with him about our loss but respected his feelings. One thing Madhu and I did talk about was having another child. We immediately stopped using birth control, and within two months I was pregnant. January of 1966 was the due date.

Our loss continued to consume us, but now we had something to look forward to and talk about as well.

part ii

Carrying On

15

Landslides in the Dodra Kwar Area

One day in August of 1965, Madhu received a telephone call from his boss saying that he needed to go on tour as soon as possible to Dodra Kwar, which was one of the most remote and backward areas of Himachal Pradesh. Several villages in this interior area of Madhu's forest division were threatened by heavy landslides. The Dodra villagers had sent a wireless message to Shimla requesting government officials to help them avert the impending disaster.

At first, Madhu was reluctant to make the trip, because we had vacation plans. Of course, he quickly realized that it was an absolute necessity and our vacation had to wait.

It was the second month of the monsoon season, so hiking to the Dodra Kwar area would be treacherous. The further-most village to be inspected was fifty-six miles from Madhu's Rohru headquarters. Fifty of the fifty-six miles were to be traveled on foot or horseback, and most of the trip was up-and-downhill. Rohru was 5,000 feet above sea level, and the highest peak to be crossed on the trip was 12,500 feet.

I was keen to go on this hiking trip. It would be lonely to stay back in Rohru after the loss of our son. But Madhu wasn't so sure it was a good idea. He pointed out that although I was used to touring with him on his forest inspection trips, this was a much more strenuous journey, and I was four months pregnant. After several heated discussions, Madhu finally agreed to let me accompany him. The trip would also include his boss, who was Conservator of Forests; the local *Tehsildar* (assistant magistrate); and an entourage of forest department staff.

On the first day of our trip to Dodra Kwar, we left Rohru at eleven in the morning. Our journey began with a six-mile jeep ride, which was just the beginning of the trip. The jeepable road from Rohru to Chirgaon Forest Rest House was fairly level. On arrival I took a short nap. After a sumptuous lunch prepared by the forestry staff at the rest house, we started on our hike up the mountain, which was the major portion of the day's journey. For this part of our journey, we had three horses, which meant most of our group travelled on foot. I rode a small brown horse; Madhu and his boss rode bigger horses. Also we had four mules to transport our luggage for the beginning of the trip. Shortly after leaving the rest house, we saw the village of Chirgaon and its famous trout fish hatchery.

We started to climb the mountain and went from 6,000 to 8,500 feet. Riding on such steep mountain trails was a new experience for Madhu and me. Several places there were mudslides (small landslides) on the trail, which made it difficult for the horses to cross with riders on their backs. The horses and mules took roundabout routes when we came to the mudslides. The first time I got down from my horse and started to walk, I felt my muscles protesting.

The animals and their handlers rejoined us where the trail was wider and clear of the mud and rocks. We all got back on our horses. As

Elma on her horse during Dodra Kwar trip

the track got steeper, I remained on my horse, but Madhu and his boss got off their horses and walked. Soon they got tired of climbing the rugged, rocky path, and they stopped to rest. I got off my horse and joined them. Some of us sat on a large boulder and others on the ground. After a short rest, we resumed the trek.

Fifteen minutes before we reached our destination, it started to rain. We didn't open our umbrellas, because we quickly learned that the mules were frantic when they saw an open umbrella, and one of the horses would stand up on his hind legs. All of us got soaked.

At six-thirty, cold and wet, we reached the Larot Forest Rest House. Its compound was full of trees with ripening red and green apples. When we walked into the old-fashioned rest house, we were greeted by two fireplaces with roaring wood fires. The *chaukidar* (caretaker) had lit them when he saw us climbing up to the rest house. Both chimneys worked well, but even if they had sent smoke into our room, I wouldn't have minded. The heat from the fire was comforting. After I had tea and the men had their drinks, we were served a delicious dinner of chicken curry, fried potatoes, lentils, and *kheer*, rice pudding. Soon after the meal, we went to bed. The day's exercise, heavy dinner, and heat from the fireplace all contributed to the soundest sleep I can remember in a long time.

The next morning, we got up early. The eighteen miles ahead of us were the toughest section of the journey. It started with a climb of nine miles from Larot up to Chancel Peak, which was 12,500 feet. There were stretches where the trail was so narrow that even I had to get down from my horse. There were no villages on the way, and the only people we met were a few laborers working on the bridle path with pickaxes.

About a half mile from Chancel Peak, we ate our pack lunch in an open area covered with bright green, mountain grass and tiny, pastel wildflowers. There were no trees, since we were above the tree line. It was a welcome change from the thick, dark forests we had been in all morning.

We sat on a brown, woolen blanket spread on the ground and used a big, flat rock for our table. But just as we started to eat lunch, it began to rain, and fog quickly moved in. Within just five minutes our view changed from a commanding scene to a sheet of mist. We couldn't even see nearby Chancel Peak.

We ate our lunch quickly, with some of the forestry staff holding umbrellas over our heads. I still felt hungry after the strenuous climb and would have liked dessert. Just a few hundred feet below us, we saw a man hurrying up the mountain with a large container on his head. As we looked carefully, we realized it was a *gujjar* carrying a huge brass pot on his head. Gujjars were the main suppliers of milk and *ghee*, clarified butter. They were a nomadic tribe of buffalo herders who brought their buffalo herds high up in the mountains for grazing during the summer months, because grass was insufficient in the plains. Before we knew it, the gujjar reached us and set his oddly shaped pot in front of us, and the rain briefly stopped.

I asked, "What does he have in the pot?"

A uniformed forest ranger replied, "I hope it's kheer."

Kheer is a sweet dessert made from milk, rice, and sugar. This Indian-style pudding is made by boiling milk slowly until it thickens, and then adding a small amount of rice. When the rice is cooked, sugar is added. During the cooking, the milk has to be continually stirred so it doesn't burn.

The gujjar proudly said in Hindi, "I have brought freshly made kheer for all of you."

In fact, our new gujjar friend had brought a lot of kheer. All twenty of us had several generous servings of the delicious, warm dessert. We finished the whole pot of rice pudding, thanked the gujjar, and started back on our journey.

In less than an hour, we reached Chancel Peak and placed wildflowers on a rock near the top of the peak. We were about to enter the Dodra Kwar area. At first, because of the rain and fog, we couldn't see into the valley. Then the rain stopped, and the fog cleared. We were amazed by the commanding view from the highest peak on our trip. I took lots of pictures with my American Agfa camera.

Gujjar giving Elma and forestry staff kheer during Dodra Kwar trip

We started down the other side of the mountain to continue our journey. The first half of our descent was quite steep, although the last half was more gradual. For me, this four-mile descent was the most difficult part of the journey. As I walked on the slippery path, I slipped and fell at least five times. Each fall was a gentle one, but it made me extremely cautious. Since I was pregnant, I descended at a snail's pace. The rain started up again and soon turned into a heavy downpour. There was no place for us to take shelter, so we kept walking.

After what seemed like an eternity, we saw two thatched roofs in the middle of nowhere. A forest guard said that they were gujjars' huts, and the gujjars were out grazing their buffaloes. Half of our party crowded into one hut and the other half into the second one. One of the men complained about the stink in the place and the dirty rug we were sitting on. For me, this primitive shelter was like a palace after our difficult descent in the pouring rain. I never expected to find a dry, warm place in the midst of the heavy rain.

At the back of the hut, I was surprised to see a skinny, black buffalo calf tied to a stake. I wondered where its mother was. Near the calf, the dying coal embers from an earlier fire kept the shelter warm and cozy. Outside the rain had almost stopped, and I knew we needed to move on.

In the light rain, we hiked down the mountain for about a mile. We could use our umbrellas now that the mules and the horses, who went wild with open umbrellas, weren't with us. Then the rain completely stopped. The path was still slippery, but I found it much easier to navigate now that I no longer needed to hold an umbrella.

By the time we reached Dodra, our resting spot for the night, the sun was shining brightly. Again we sat in a rest house by a blazing wood fire. I guessed that today's journey was probably the toughest and most tiring part of our whole trip. I certainly hoped so. We had climbed from 8,500 feet up to 12,500 and back down to 8,500 feet.

The Dodra area was the first place we visited that was threatened by a landslide. After a night's rest, Madhu, his boss, the forestry staff, and the Tehsildar left to inspect the problem. They wanted to see what could be done to stop the landslide which, the villagers were afraid would turn into a much larger landslide. I stayed back at the rest house. The landslide was a short walk, and they were back in two hours. I overheard Madhu and his Conservator discussing what they saw. The problem seemed to be caused by the cultivation of crops on the steep slopes.

Madhu suggested, "We need to teach the villagers to use step farming."

Another cause of the landslide was the excessive grazing of goats and sheep on the mountain. All the villagers kept large flocks of goats and sheep, because they couldn't make a living and feed their families by only growing grains, lentils, and potatoes. The area was so mountainous that farming was not profitable. The sheep—with their dirty wool—and the skinny goats augmented their earnings and provided food for them.

After lunch we pushed off to Kwar, which was only six miles away. The path to Kwar was narrow, rocky, and treacherous in places. Since we no longer had the mules, we had to find some people to carry our rations, sleeping gear, and clothes. With difficulty, we persuaded a few villagers to carry our luggage. The men in this area were lazy about doing manual work. They were content with their lives and had little interest in improving their poor living standard. The women did most of the work in the fields, gathered wood, and did all of the housework. Men did take the animals out to graze. When the forest department required laborers on a daily wage basis, there were almost as many women as men who took the jobs.

From Dodra we climbed down the mountain to Rupen River, which was about 6,000 feet above sea level. We crossed the Rupen River on a thirty-foot-long, swaying, wooden bridge that was three feet wide and had no railings. While crossing the swaying bridge, I was afraid to look down at the rushing water below, but I had to because there were stones on the bridge, which I didn't want to trip over. The stones covered holes where the timber planks had rotted. When I reached the other side safely, I sat down and watched the others cross in single file. I was relieved to make it across without feeling dizzy.

Narrow bridge on Dodra Kwar trip

Half our journey to Kwar was complete. A three-mile ascent to Kwar at 8,500 feet remained. The climb wasn't much after yesterday's tough journey. Along the way, we stopped at a retired forest guard's apple orchard. In the midst of the orchard, he had built a compact house that was freshly whitewashed. The house was surrounded by sunflowers, roses, and apple trees laden with red, green, and yellow apples. The guard asked us to pick as many apples as we wanted.

While sitting in the house and munching on a juicy apple, I asked in Hindi, "What do you do with all these apples?"

He replied, "My family and friends eat what we can, which is a small percentage of the crop. Then we dry the rest of the apples and feed them to the cows throughout the year."

I was shocked to hear that the cows were eating all these apples, which sold in Delhi or Bombay for one to three rupees[26] per apple.

The guard told us, "By the time I pay laborers to carry wooden crates of apples to Rohru so they can be shipped by truck to markets throughout India, there is no profit. Someday there will be a motorized road, but I don't expect it to happen during my lifetime."

For the time being, those were some very lucky cows.

When we reached Kwar, we were greeted by villagers and a local band that was part of a *mela* (local fair). The enthusiasm of the villagers with their dancing and singing spread to our group of forest officials. The village leader approached us. He bowed his head, held his hands as though praying, and said, "Namaste-ji."

Then he spoke to Madhu in Hindi. "Do you know that your wife is probably the first foreigner to visit this area?"

I wasn't surprised. Foreigners were uncommon even in the urban, easily accessible areas of Himachal Pradesh in the 1960s, so it was unlikely that they would reach such a far-off, unknown area.

The village leader explained, "We slaughtered a couple of goats in honor of your visit to the village. Some of the goat meat will be given to your cooks, and the rest distributed to our villagers."

The next day was a rest day for me. I spent the day at the inspection hut where we were staying, while the men went to Jaka. It was almost a six mile hike going and six miles returning. Jaka was the site of the furthermost landslide to be inspected. The landslide had started during this year's rainy season, and according to reports, it was extremely dangerous.

The men were expected back at Kwar around five for tea. As I wait-

---

[26] Twenty to forty cents per apple

ed for them, I read for a while and then napped, a habit I followed whenever possible throughout my pregnancy.

Of course, I couldn't nap for the entire day, and being alone gave me plenty of time to think of Raju, which made me sad. I realized it would have been even harder if I had stayed home by myself. I needed a distraction. When I heard drums and flutes and saw people dancing in a nearby open field, I decided to visit the fair on my own. I walked to the mela and was offered a place to sit with the local ladies on a blanket spread on the ground. According to their customs, the ladies and men sat separately for social functions.

The fair quickly became animated with the arrival of the local *devtas*, large, stuffed figures of gods and goddesses. The devtas were dressed in bright clothes with lots of jewelry and were carried on *palkis*, stretcher-like arrangements with cloth canopy rooftops. Each devta was carried by two men who held the two poles supporting the platform on which the devta was perched. The platform was decorated with brightly colored pieces of velvet and shiny, silk cloth. Often the devtas and the platforms bounced up and down and swayed from side to side. The local people said that the actions of the gods and goddesses were not controlled by the men carrying them; instead, they believed that the devtas controlled their own movements. Frequently, they told me, a devta was so violent that the men carrying the palki had difficulty holding the poles.

I had trouble believing that the devtas caused all this frantic action. Once in a while, however, my imagination did get the better of me, and I sensed a devta was alive. I had to remind myself that they were only replicas.

Then the lively folk dancing began, accompanied by a loud, honking, screeching band. Singing and folk dancing were popular in the mountains. At the fairs men and women danced together, which was unusual for some parts of India. I watched a group of male and female dancers in a circle formation, as they joined hands in a crossed-arm fashion. The leader was at the head of the circle, dipping and swaying, while he motioned the others to join him. One section of the circle was left open for new dancers to join the group. The dancing and singing, which started in the afternoon, lasted late into the night.

People were exchanging *burfi*, Indian sweets, and puffed rice candies. I learned while watching others that when offered condiments, it was customary to give a sweet of your own or money in return. I was a little embarrassed that I had nothing to offer in return for the sweets

I was given. As the day progressed, the men began to drink a lot of home-brewed liquor. Only a few women drank the strong-smelling liquor, but quite a few helped with the brewing. Many homes had their own distilleries, even though making liquor at home was illegal.

During mela time, the villagers wore new clothes or their best clothes, which they had saved for this occasion. In fact, it was one of the few times people washed their clothes, a task that, along with taking showers, was quite limited since there was no running water in the houses. Water had to be carried from a nearby, mountain stream and then heated, which meant that extra firewood had to be gathered.

These villagers didn't bathe on a daily basis, although that was done in many places in India. Even during the summer months, many wore dark clothes, which were made from a hand-woven, woolen fabric.

I asked one woman in Hindi, "Aren't you feeling hot in your black, woolen coat?"

She said in Hindi, "No, I'm not."

I asked, "What do you wear in the winter to keep warm, if you wear so many warm clothes in the summer?"

"I might put on another sweater, but that's all."

The women's jewelry was elaborate. Some wore gold, but most wore silver. Each piece was heavy and showy. Jewelry included the usual rings, necklaces, bracelets, and earrings, but there were also less common pieces, such as silver belts. I noticed that the village women wore sets of earrings, bracelets, and necklaces—sometimes as many as twelve pieces in a set. One woman had each ear pierced in six places. Often the earrings were so heavy that their earlobes drooped. Their ankle bracelets made a tinkling sound. I saw one woman wearing a silver nose ring with a pendant the size of a half dollar coin and wondered if it didn't interfere with her eating.

All of the women wore something on their heads. The most common headgear was a hand-woven, woolen scarf. Often a *pahari topi*, a soft woolen pillbox type of hat popular in the mountains, was worn on top of the scarf. Usually only men wore these pahari caps, but here they were worn by men and women. A few women wore *dupattas*, long head scarves. I learned that these were the younger women who had gone to Delhi the previous year to perform their local folk dances at the Republic Day celebration on January 26. Their trip had been sponsored by the central government, so that people in the plains could see what dancing in the interior hills of Himachal Pradesh was like.

After a couple of hours at the fair, I thought that I should return to the forest inspection hut to see if the men were back. They didn't reach the inspection hut until eight in the evening. I listened to them talk about the trip. They felt that it was worthwhile and discussed plans for preventing further landslides. Some of the steeper areas would have to be closed to cultivation and grazing. In the reduced cultivated areas, the villagers needed to make terraced fields and drainage ditches.

Madhu mentioned, "As soon as I get back to Rohru, I will send a team of forest guards and laborers to help with the landslides and to implement terracing for step farming."

On a larger scale the Conservator said, "I will ask for funding from the H.P. government to do extensive projects to help save the villages from further landslides."

This discussion continued throughout the evening.

On August 14 we spent the day at Kwar, and it was a well-deserved rest for the men before we started our trek home. By afternoon, however, the men were feeling restless. They saw the fair going on below, and with a little urging from a group of village leaders, we were led to the mela by a four-piece band. Chairs were carried for us from the inspection hut. We sat on the chairs and watched the dancing and singing.

It wasn't long before some young women came up to us and asked in Hindi, "Please dance with us."

One by one our group members joined the dancing. The Conservator and Tehsildar didn't dance at first, but with persuasion, they joined in. Most of us picked up the dances quickly, and I soon felt part of the large dancing circle. The steps were simple and repetitious. The only difference was that sometimes the steps were done slowly and other times much faster. After our dancing session, we sat in our chairs, and some local women with long, black, braided hair brought us burfi and puffed rice candies. Finally, we ended our evening of village mela fun and went back to the inspection hut for dinner.

Our return trip started on Independence Day, and the weather was clear. Along the way we could see where one of the landslides threatened the village. When we were in the open areas, the views were spectacular. We had missed many of these lovely views at the start of our hike because of the rain and fog. Again we crossed the swaying bridge with holes and stones on it where the wood was rotting. I was relieved when the bridge crossing was behind us.

Just before we reached Dodra, a loud, local band greeted us. The band consisted of a drummer who was beating a kitchen pan with a large spoon and three other drummers with more conventional drums.

Two of the drummers had shoulder-length hair. The band played loud music and led us up to the rest house and then to the local mela. Today we saw something new. There were a few children who dressed themselves as horses. They crouched down on all fours, covered their backs with a blanket, and wore masks that looked like horses' heads. These horses tried to disrupt the dancers, and their horseplay got wilder and wilder. As it started to get dark, the horses calmed down. Some men lit kerosene lamps for us, but we decided it was time to go back to the rest house.

The next day we left for Chirgaon, the end of our long hike. When we returned, I said a silent prayer, thankful for our safe return from the remote mountains and valleys in the extreme interior of Himachal Pradesh. Even as I looked forward to the days ahead, I knew I would always treasure this memorable adventure.

American and Indian Deliveries

After three years in India and a postponed trip to the United States, Madhu and I decided it was time for me to visit my parents. I would go first, and he would follow after four months, when he was due for some time off.

I was six months pregnant when I arrived at my parents' home in Birmingham, Michigan. The reunion involved mixed feelings. We were happy to be together, but it was hard for me to be returning alone. I was meeting them seven months after the death of Raju, their first grandchild, whom they had seen only in pictures.

Shortly after my arrival in Birmingham, I started working at temporary jobs to pay for my hospital expenses, and I continued to work up until my delivery. When the labor pains started, I called in sick.

At the time, my youngest sister, Barbara, and I were staying with a neighbor, Mrs. Eddy, because our parents had gone to New Jersey to make funeral arrangements for our grandmother. Mrs. Eddy rushed me to the hospital. The staff at the front desk asked a few questions, and in a short time an attendant helped me onto a rolling stretcher cart and pushed me to the labor room.

The doctor on duty asked a few more questions. He realized that I was in a lot of pain, so he gave me a spinal. Once the spinal took effect, I was hardly aware of what was happening. Finally, he said, "Congratulations! You have a seven-pound, thirteen-ounce baby girl."

As I looked at my daughter, I was overcome with joy. Mrs. Eddy and Barbara came into the delivery room to see us. They kept saying how beautiful the new baby was.

Unlike my first birthing experience in India, where our baby slept in a large room with me and my mother-in-law also stayed there as my attendant, this time baby daughter was carried by a nurse to a nursery, and I was taken to a small, semi-private room, where I was helped into bed. There was a screen separating my bed from a second patient's bed. I immediately took a short nap. A nurse came in the room as I woke up and said that I had a phone call. It was Mrs. Eddy, who told me that Mom and Dad were coming back from New Jersey the next morning.

When my doctor came by in the morning, he examined me and asked me how I was feeling. When I told him that I felt good, he asked, "Do you want to go home today?" He explained, "Usually I keep mother and baby for at least three days, but since you don't have insurance, this is your second delivery, and you have help at home, you can be discharged today if you like."

I thankfully said, "Yes, I'd like to go home."

Before leaving the hospital, I had to decide on a name for baby daughter, not like India, where I had to wait thirteen days before naming Raju. I decided on Tara Elizabeth Vaidya. Tara was the name of one of our good Indian friends in Durham, North Carolina, and Elizabeth was my middle name. A nurse brought Tara to me for a try at breastfeeding. We worked on it. After Tara was taken back to the nursery, another nurse came to give me a sponge bath. It seemed like someone was there even before I needed to ring a bell for help.

That evening my parents came to the hospital to take Tara and me home. They were delighted to see their granddaughter. Mother held Tara. Looking closely at her, she said, "How lovely."

Then we packed up and went home. When we got there, Mom carried Tara upstairs

Tara and Louise, my mother, in Birmingham, Michigan

and put her in a bassinette in the room across the hall from my bedroom. For a baby to sleep alone in a separate room was unacceptable in India. Here it was okay. I left the door open between my bedroom and Tara's bedroom across the hall.

Taking care of a baby in America was different than in India, where my mother-in-law took charge and cared for our son in her own way. This time, my parents and sister were there to help as needed, but I was in charge. When asked they made suggestions, but otherwise I bathed, fed, and took Tara to her doctor visits on my own.

After Tara was born, my mother encouraged me to write about my Indian experiences. She found out about a writing course at the Birmingham Community House and strongly suggested that I sign up for the course which I did.[27] Mother and Barbara took care of Tara when I went to my writing classes and never complained that she cried a lot while I was gone.

Madhu came to Birmingham two months after Tara was born. When he saw her, his face lit up in his signature smile, which I hadn't seen since Raju's death. He held Tara and rocked her in his arms. She smiled back at him.

The next three months went by quickly. During the day, Madhu helped with outdoor work and cooking. Once again, my family called him Steve. I attended my writing classes and worked on my memoir. Evenings we played bridge with my parents. If Tara was awake, my sister Barbara played with her.

When Tara turned five months old, the three of us returned to India. Soon after our return, Madhu was transferred from Rohru to Kulu, which was a much bigger town. We had a spacious government house in a forest colony with ten other forest officers living nearby. Our Kulu posting was a better place for me than Rohru. I had a large circle of friends, and many of the women spoke English.

Madhu, George (my Dad), and Elma in Birmingham, Michigan

---

[27] Some of the early chapters of my memoir were composed for the class.

By the time Tara was a year old, Madhu and I decided that we wanted another child, so we stopped using birth control. I soon became pregnant, with a due date just after Christmas.

Christmas day we had a tea party at our home for our Kulu friends. I made American snacks to serve with tea. There were sandwiches, French fries, deviled eggs, cookies, and cake. Looking very pregnant, I greeted the guests as we wished each other Merry Christmas. After everyone left, I felt exhausted and let the servant clean up so I could go to bed.

Early the next morning my labor pains started. I knew that this was for real, since it was my third time around. Madhu and I packed my things to go to the hospital. He called Ama-ji in Mandi and asked her to come to Kulu to help out. It was a two-hour bus ride from Mandi to Kulu, but she said that she would reach Kulu by early afternoon. Then we woke up Tara, who was almost two years old, got her dressed, and called a neighbor to come and take care of her. As soon as the neighbor arrived, Madhu and I left for the hospital in his jeep, a five-minute ride.

Once at the hospital I was directed to a room off to one side of the main hospital. A nurse led me to a room with a delivery table. Madhu was asked to wait outside on an open porch. The nurse asked me if I was okay with a midwife doing the delivery. I told her that I wanted a doctor. She said, "We only have male doctors, and most women prefer a female midwife."

I requested, "Please ask Dr. Avninder Singh to do the delivery." Dr. Singh was our family doctor.

The nurse promised to call him and had me lie down on the delivery table. My pains were now five minutes apart and quite intense. Dr. Avninder Singh arrived and with little conversation proceeded with the delivery. Being my third one, things went quickly and our second daughter was born.

After baby and I were cleaned up, we moved to a room next to the rudimentary delivery room. This tiny room looked like a storage room, with burlap bags piled up along one wall, but at least it did have a bed. I decided that I wanted to go home as soon as they would release me.

When I asked for a baby scale, they said that they didn't have one. They brought a regular scale and had me get on it with baby and then by myself. After subtracting the difference, we had an approximate weight of seven pounds.

Ama-ji arrived early that afternoon and made sure that food and drinks were sent from home for me. Dr. Singh met with Ama-ji and suggested that I spend one night in the hospital. However, I insisted on going home that evening. He finally agreed.

Before we left, I made a few attempts at breastfeeding and ate an early dinner. Then Madhu and Ama-ji packed our few belongings. In five minutes, we were home. When we arrived, Tara ran over and gave me a big hug. Now that I was home, she followed me around and wanted me to take care of her rather than Ama-ji.

I asked Ama-ji to put our little one in a bassinette in the room next to my bedroom. She wasn't too happy about baby and mother sleeping in separate rooms but finally agreed. This time I decided that I was going to negotiate with Ama-ji about our differences in childrearing.

Three hospital deliveries, all were very different. At Shimla, a lady doctor did the delivery in a well-equipped delivery room, and then baby and I were moved to a spacious room with an attached bathroom and a bed for me and one for my attendant. In America, no family attendant stayed in my small, modern, semi-private hospital room. At Kulu, I was in a makeshift room separate from the main hospital, and it was my shortest stay in a hospital. But the main thing was that in each case the baby and I were cared for, healthy, and safe.

17

Wait—Wait—Wait

After almost five years of living in India, I still wasn't quite used to the frequent waits.

It was late May of 1968, and Madhu was posted at Kulu, where he was Divisional Forest Officer. Now that we had two young girls, two-and-a-half-year-old Tara and six-month-old Rita, I did not accompany him on his tours as much as I did when we had only one child.

Madhu's most recent tour was to Manali, where a group of tourist huts were being built by the forest department. He was to return late in the afternoon. I was waiting for the sound of his jeep to pull into the compound in front of our government house. The doorbell rang.

I opened the front door and was surprised to see his head clerk, who had come on foot from the office. He informed me, "Your husband's jeep had an accident, but he's okay. They are bringing him to the Kulu Government Hospital to check him out."

I anxiously asked, "Are you sure he's okay? What happened?"

"I don't know the details, but your husband and the driver are okay. Once they get to the hospital, I'll send a jeep to take you there."

I later learned that the accident happened near Raison, halfway between Kulu and Manali. It was raining heavily. The driver rounded a sharp curve and saw a truck coming right at them, so he slammed on the brakes. The jeep skidded out of control and hit a rock along the inner edge of the road.

While waiting for the office jeep to pick me up, I asked my neighbor to come over and watch Tara and Rita. We had a servant in the house, but I didn't like leaving them alone with him. After a nerve-racking wait, the jeep came to take me to the hospital.

On arriving at the hospital, I was led into the emergency room, where I saw Madhu being treated by a doctor. He had a cut above his eye and several bruises on his face. He gave me a weak smile as the doctor stitched his forehead.

The doctor informed me, "I put five stitches on the forehead cut. I suspect his leg is broken, and we will take an X-ray tomorrow morning. I gave him painkillers for his stay in the hospital tonight."

As soon as the doctor finished checking for more injuries, they took Madhu on a stretcher to a large private room on the second floor. When we reached the room, he was lifted into his bed.

I held his hand and asked, "How do you feel?"

He looked at me, and I saw the uncertainty in his eyes. "I hope the painkillers start working soon. My leg really hurts. I'm worried about the results of tomorrow's X-ray."

The next morning they X-rayed his leg. The upper portion of his right leg between his knee and hip was broken. In fact, the femur bone was broken into two separate parts. The doctor told us, "His leg will have to be put in traction until the two bones are pulled back into place and calcify. Then a plaster cast will be put on. The traction period will mean at least a six-week hospital stay."

As soon as Madhu's parents heard about the accident, they came to Kulu with Madhu's grandmother and other close relatives. After their arrival, we discussed moving Madhu to a larger hospital—possibly Chandigarh, Delhi, or Shimla.

Our doctor said, "We need to wait to decide about moving him until after they take X-rays again in five to six days."

Madhu was still in a lot of pain, even with the painkillers and sleeping pills, but he insisted that he wanted to stay at the Kulu hospital.

I went back and forth from the hospital and the house but spent as much time at the hospital as I could. My mother-in-law, Ama-ji, took care of Tara and Rita at home. Tara made a lot of hospital visits, but Rita came only a couple of times. Once I was comfortable with Ama-ji taking care of the girls, I occasionally spent the night at the hospital. All of Madhu's meals were cooked at home and brought to him in a stainless steel *tiffan* carrier.

During the day, Madhu's father spent a lot of time in Madhu's room, which was large enough for at least five visitors. At that time smoking was allowed in the hospital room, and Madhu was a smoker. However, according to Indian customs, he didn't smoke in front of his elders, especially his father, Babu-ji. When Madhu felt the urge to smoke, we made excuses to get Babu-ji out of the room. After we did this a couple of times, Babu-ji realized what was going on, and he made excuses on his own to leave. He stayed away long enough for Madhu to finish his cigarette.

Eight weeks passed, and the doctors started to talk about putting on a plaster cast. Monsoon season was in full swing, and our doctor who was very cautious wanted to put the cast on when the rains slowed down so as to avoid any infection.

Finally, the monsoons diminished and the nine-week wait was over. Madhu's leg was taken out of traction, and a plaster cast was put on. It started on his foot and went up to his waist. On July 30, the day after the cast was put on, he came home from the hospital in a pickup truck and was carried into the house by our servants and a driver.

Tara and Rita playing with their American plastic sewing machine

When Tara saw her Daddy brought into the house, she cried out in a singsong voice, "Oh, my daddy's come home, my daddy, my daddy."

It was a relief to have Madhu at home, even when he was confined to bed and complained about the itching under the huge cast. My in-laws planned to leave the following week. The guest load would lessen once they left. The number of visiting relatives had been unbelievable. Practically everybody who came to inquire about Madhu was invited to have a meal or spend a couple of days. Most accepted.

On August 28, Madhu's leg was X-rayed with the cast on. The doctors felt the progress was good, and after two weeks they planned to take the cast off and X-ray again. If they thought his bone was weight-bearing, they would keep the cast off. Otherwise, they would put another cast on. We crossed our fingers that all would go well. It had been a long time since the accident occurred, with constant waiting periods between each step of the recovery.

The second week of September, the cast was taken off, and Madhu was X-rayed again. The doctors were pleased with the results. Not only were the broken bone parts joined together, but both legs were the same length, which had been another potential cause for concern. We were delighted that they didn't need to put a second cast on. Madhu had to stay in bed for a week more with as little movement as possible, but after one week he could start bending his injured leg.

Finally, on October 1, Madhu sat up, moved his leg, and turned over in bed. So far, the doctors had said that he shouldn't walk. In another week, they would take another X-ray and give their verdict of when he could start walking.

The X-ray was taken, and the doctors gave Madhu the okay to use crutches, which he started to use cautiously. In a week, he was back to work. He went to the office in the morning and worked from home in the afternoon. The doctor said that he had another two weeks on crutches. I figured it would be at least four weeks. I added a week or two to whatever dates the doctors said. They never kept their word with dates. It was always a waiting game.

Tara and Rita painting our Kulu house fence

Tara and Rita in forestry jeep at Kulu

18

My First Teaching Job in India

From the time I was young, I loved teaching. When Madhu was transferred to Chamba, Himachal Pradesh in 1971, I received my first offer to follow this passion in India.

At the time, five-year-old daughter, Tara, needed to be admitted to school. Fortunately, Chamba townspeople, headed by Sagar Chand Nayar, had recently opened an English-medium school named Bharatiya Public School. The name was misleading, since it was a private school. All the other schools in town were government schools, operated and staffed by the state of Himachal Pradesh. Their medium of instruction was Hindi.

Bharatiya Public School yearbook

When I took Tara for her admission to Bharatiya Public School, which was located in the first floor of a recreational clubhouse, it was a bright sunny day. We arrived at the school and saw many students playing on the lawn in front of the large stone building. In the evenings, there would be badminton games, card-playing sessions, and other social activities in the two-story clubhouse.

My First Teaching Job in India

We went into the principal's sparsely furnished office and were greeted by a short man with a black mustache and sideburns. He stood up and introduced himself. His tone commanded respect.

I introduced myself and explained, "I'm here for my daughter's admission to kindergarten. Tara was studying in Kulu at a private English-medium school."

The principal asked several questions. Then, he said that he was pleased to admit Tara to his school. Next, he wanted to know where I was from originally. When I told him that I was born and raised in the United States, he asked, "Are you interested in teaching at our school?"

"I might be, but not until next year when my younger daughter starts school."

"How old is she?"

"Rita is three."

"She's a little young, but I'll admit her to our nursery class if you'd like."

"Thanks, but I don't want her to start school until she's four."

I guessed that he really wanted me as a teacher in his school, which made sense. I was a foreigner, and my first language was English.

A year later I took Rita for her admission to the nursery class. Again the principal mentioned, "I have an opening for a teacher. Are you available?"

"I might be interested. What class is it?"

"It would be for the third standard (grade).[28] I teach the highest standard, which is a combined fourth and fifth standard class."

Then he showed me around the school. We walked into the first standard classroom, and all thirty students stood up and said, "Good morning, Ma'am."

Next we went into a smaller room. There was a curtain partitioning the room into two classrooms. On one side of the partition were six students busy talking, but when they saw us, there was absolute silence. The class on the other side of the partition had two teenage boys, who were writing in their notebooks.

When we left the divided classroom, the principal said, "If you accept the job you will have the classroom with the six students, and my class is the one with two students."

We went back to his office and discussed salaries. He explained, "I

---

[25]In India the classes in schools are called standards, equivalent to grades in America. Third standard would be equivalent to third grade in America.

pay local Chamba teachers one hundred and fifty rupees a month, and those who come from Delhi or other places in India receive a starting pay of three hundred rupees a month. You would receive one hundred and fifty rupees[29] since you already live in Chamba."

I was disappointed with his offer and told him so. "You may consider me a local teacher because I am living in Chamba at this time, but I am from the United States. I will be the only teacher in the school whose first language is English. In America, I completed twelve years of school and two years of college. This was equivalent to an Indian undergraduate degree."

He listened and then said, "Okay, I'll pay you three hundred rupees[30] a month." He must have figured that a foreign teacher would attract more admissions.

I accepted the job and was told to start the next day. Before leaving, I requested the third standard English and math books. I took them home with me, and that evening I enthusiastically prepped for my first teaching job in India.

The next day Tara, Rita, and I walked a half mile up a steep hill to the school. As we walked through the section where shoemakers worked and lived, several kids called out, "Hippie, hippie."

I realized that these children, playing on the narrow road, had limited experiences with foreigners. Their contact was with the hippies, who visited Chamba in the late sixties and seventies. Many of the hippies came for the opium that was freely available.

Of course, I certainly wasn't a narcotic-loving hippie just because I came from America, and Tara and Rita, who grew up in India, were certainly not hippies! I was upset about the girls and I being called hippies. I wanted the girls to know that this was not true, and I told them that they were Indian-Americans.

When we arrived at school, the girls went to their classrooms, and I took my books to my small, bare classroom. A bell rang and I went out to the front lawn. Students and teachers were lined up by classes for the morning assembly. The principal led the group in prayers and the pledge to the Indian flag. Then he made announcements for the day and introduced me as the new American teacher. He dismissed the students to their classrooms, and I walked with my six students to our room.

I entered the classroom and realized I was nervous, particularly

---

[29] About eight dollars

[30] About sixteen dollars

knowing that the principal was teaching in the other half of the partitioned room. My students sat quietly in their wooden chairs. I asked questions, but no one replied at first.

Then one boy stood up and said, "My name is Rajeev, and this is my first time in an English-medium school."

Once he spoke, the others lost their shyness and told me that they were learning English for the first time and were afraid they would make mistakes when they talked.

I assured them, "It's okay to make mistakes."

There were two girls and four boys in my class. They had on school uniforms. Girls wore brown, pleated skirts, and boys wore brown shorts that reached a little above their knees. All had on white dress shirts with maroon and yellow Bharatiya Public School neckties. Two of the students were Chamba residents, and their parents owned shops in town. Another boy's father was a Public Works Department contractor from the state of Punjab. The other parents were posted here as government officials.

Elma with her third standard Bharatiya Public School students

As the school year progressed, I became involved in writing and directing a school play. It was based on the story "Snow White and the Seven Dwarfs." Many students tried out for parts, including Rita and Tara, so I asked the other teachers to choose the cast. Tara was chosen to be Snow White, and Rita was picked to be one of the seven dwarfs. Most of the students in my class were chosen to be dwarfs. We practiced every day, and a female teacher made costumes for the actors and actresses. She stitched matching tunics and hats for the seven dwarfs. Also, she made a crown and a long white dress for Tara.

Students knew their lines well, but many spoke softly. I tried to encourage them. "Speak louder so your audience will hear each and every line. Even with the microphone, you have to speak up."

A chorus of students shouted, "Is this better?"

Finally, we were ready to perform for an audience. The program was held on the front lawn of the school. Rows of chairs were set up for the guests. There was a tent, where the special invitees sat. One of them

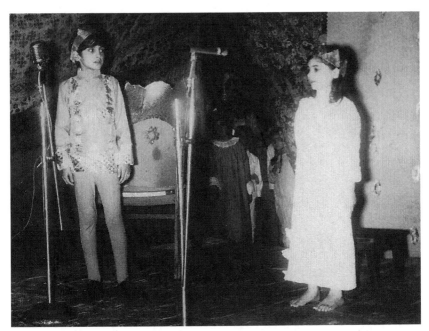

Rajeev and Tara in Snow White drama

was a local political minister, who gave a short speech congratulating the school on its good work. Besides the performance of our "Snow White" drama, there were local songs and folk dances. The audience of parents, students, teachers, and Chamba residents clapped loudly for all the presentations. Judging by the complimentary comments made by the guests as they left, the program was a huge success.

Thirty-five years later, I have reconnected with some of my Bharatiya Public School students through Facebook and phone calls. They are living in the United States, Canada, Australia, and India. One of the students, a successful career woman, recently visited me at my home in the United States, and we reminisced about our memorable school experiences. She still called me "Ma'am," as she did when she was my third standard student.

part III

Visits from American Family

15

Mother's First Impressions of Delhi

My mother left Detroit on January 30, 1975 for her first visit to India. She had scrimped and saved to make this trip to visit me and my family. She had sold an antique doll to help pay for the $500 round-trip ticket. Her cleaning woman, Dessie Mae, had agreed to take six months off from her weekly cleaning job (every Wednesday) at my parents' Birmingham home to help Mother save money.

The Pan Am flight made many stops on the way to Delhi. The first stop was Boston, and then London, where, Mother later told me, it seemed she had to walk for miles. Next was Frankfort and then Karachi, a desolate-looking airport. She was held up there, because the Delhi airport was fogged in. After a ninety-minute delay, the plane finally took off.

When my mother entered the Delhi airport, she went through immigration and customs. As she unlocked her suitcase,

A page from Mother's journal from her first trip to India

Mother's First Impressions of Delhi

the uniformed customs official said that she didn't need to open it, and he waved her on. There were many policeman in the airport. Another passenger told her that they were there because Mrs. Indira Gandhi, the Prime Minister of India, had just left on a plane to Agra.

When Mother walked out of the customs area, she had to wait for me. Five minutes later, I rushed over and gave her a big hug. I quickly explained, "We are late, because I called the airport and was told the flight was delayed by two hours. When I called back, they said that the flight had landed."

Then Steve hugged my mother, while Tara and Rita hid behind me. I stepped aside and told them, "Say *hi* to Grandmother."

They each shyly said, "Hi."

My mother had never seen Rita, and she had not seen Tara since she was five months old. Now they were nine and seven years old

Mother said, "Elma, you look much older. I think it's because your face is thinner. Why is Steve wearing a cap?"

We laughed, and I explained that he had cut his own hair and made a mess. He took his cap off, and I showed Mother several bald spots.

From the airport, we rode to the home of the Gupta family, where we were staying. They were longtime friends from the time we were posted at Kulu, and they vacationed there. Their home was in Sundernager, a posh area of Delhi. My sister Virginia had also stayed there when she visited me in 1968. Their house was convenient for sightseeing and shopping. They always invited us to stay with them when we visited Delhi.

As soon as we got to the house, I took Mother to meet Mrs. Meenakshi Gupta, who was in bed. She was a pretty woman but quite sick. I guessed that she might be suffering from female issues or bouts of depression, but it was unclear. Mother was embarrassed that we were staying with them when Mrs. Gupta was sick. But every time we suggested that we leave, Mrs. Gupta said in her melodious voice, "No problem, no problem."

From her bedroom, we were shown to our rooms. We had the whole second floor to ourselves. The bathroom lights didn't work at first, so Mother took out a flashlight that she had brought from the United States as a gift for Steve's family.

We freshened up and went downstairs. Mr. Y.N. Gupta amused Mother. He was well-dressed in his American-looking clothes, but over them he wore a camel-colored Indian shawl, which he wrapped around his shoulders. He almost always wore this pashmina shawl, because at this time of year, the house was cold all the time. The family used a small, electric space heater in the living room. The other rooms had no heating arrangement so a couple of space heaters were moved from room to room as needed. During the day, it was quite warm outside in the sun, but not in the house.

The Guptas had three children. Ajay was a chubby ten-year-old who liked to roughhouse with the girls, which annoyed Mrs. Gupta. Anjali, their sixteen-year-old daughter, was very pretty and friendly. Mother loved the way she always started her conversations respectfully with "Mrs. Griscom." I think Mother related to Sanjay who was eighteen, and wanted to go to Dartmouth College, which his dad had attended. All the kids spoke fluent English and talked freely with Mother. They had three dogs. The beagle and another tiny dog ran in and out of the house. The giant Saint Bernard stayed outside. Mother wondered how the Saint Bernard survived in the Delhi summer heat.

There were several servants to do the housework and cooking. They were always in the house. The servants sat on the kitchen floor to do the prep work. When they weren't working, they huddled in a corner of the kitchen. Mother was afraid that she might trip over them when she went into the kitchen. I had no problem with the servants and supervised them when they made her special food, which usually was soup and sandwiches. Mother couldn't eat the spicy Indian food that the rest of us ate.

Shortly after arriving, we went upstairs, and Mother showed us some of the gifts she had brought for us. Tara and Rita loved the clothes, puzzles, books, and plastic jump ropes she brought for them. They still were too shy to speak with her, but the smiles on their faces showed their appreciation.

After the gift giving, Steve told Mother that he had to leave on the evening train for a forest auction at Pathankot where timber from his work area was being sold. He would be meeting us there, after we finished our shopping in Delhi and our sightseeing trips to Agra and Jaipur. This was my first trip to Jaipur. I was totally in charge and wasn't sure of what to expect.

25

Visit to Jaipur

On Sunday morning, Mother, Tara, Rita, and I left the spacious home of the Gupta family to catch the seven-thirty bus to Jaipur, which departed from the Lodhi Hotel in central Delhi. When we reached the hotel, the doorman was sitting next to a small electric heater at the entrance. There were huge, colorful pansies growing in front of the hotel. We had breakfast in the crowded lobby while waiting for the bus, which was late.

Finally, the deluxe bus arrived, and we all got on and sat in our assigned seats. Mother asked me, "Why is it called *deluxe*, when there are scratches on the outside of the bus and rips on the seats?"

I told her that it was much better than an ordinary bus.

During the ride, we went through many poor villages with small, dilapidated wooden houses. At our first rest stop, everyone rushed to get off the bus. As we walked around the village, young children followed us and begged us to let them shine our shoes. We only escaped them when we went to the bathroom, which Mother called the *john*. She thought the bathroom was horrible.

While others had tea and breakfast, we watched. I wouldn't let any of us eat the food in the tiny, open-air, roadside restaurant. I was afraid that it might make us sick. Instead, we ate the snacks we had brought with us.

A peanut vendor approached us, and Tara and Rita begged me to buy them peanuts. I agreed and bought the peanuts, which were packed in a bag made from recycled newspapers. They immediately started eating the peanuts and throwing the shells on the ground. I didn't see any trashcans.

Back on the road, we saw mountains in the distance, and the land along the roadside appeared arid. Mother wondered how people eked out an existence from the small farms along the way. Only a few of the farms were irrigated. I saw scarecrows in some of the fields. The mountains got taller and looked like big rocks. There were ancient forts on some of them.

After six hours, we finally entered Jaipur through the city gates. The streets were crowded with oxcarts, motorcycles, scooters, bicycles, three-wheelers, taxis, cars, buses, trucks, and street vendors pushing their wagons. It was wild, with people driving at terrific speeds, changing lanes, and constantly blowing horns. Mother wasn't used to this kind of traffic. She looked tense.

Our first stop was the tourist bureau in central Jaipur. I wanted to check the rates at available hotels. Our Delhi host had suggested that we stay at the Rambagh Palace, which was a five-star hotel located just outside the city, but I favored staying in a downtown hotel. Both the tourist officer and our taxi driver suggested the Emerald Hotel in central downtown. We went to the hotel, and I went in by myself. I returned to the taxi and said, "The place looks great, and the price is reasonable."

Hotel employees unloaded our luggage, and we followed them up to our room. When we went inside, I noticed a disappointed look on Mother's face. I asked her, "What's wrong?"

She said, "I wish we had stayed at Rambagh Palace. Things look crummy here, but I can stand it." She didn't like the lobby, the bathroom, and the beds in our room. For me, they were what I was used to.

The next morning, we took a sightseeing bus to see the city of Jaipur. On the bus, Mother took out her knitting, which involved round needles. Tara and Rita also knew how to knit, but they had never seen round needles. She let them try the needles, which broke the ice, and they lost their shyness with her.

After sightseeing, we had lunch. When Mother saw Rita eating rice with her fingers, she was shocked. I told her this was a common practice for Indians.

Following lunch, we went for a walk in town. The walking paths were crowded with people. Tara and Rita had brought along the jump ropes, which were a gift from Mother. As they skipped rope on our

Visit to Jaipur

walk, local kids followed us. They all wanted to try the American jump ropes with plastic handles. We almost had a fight on our hands, as the city children kept begging to use the ropes.

We went in several shops and bought a bedspread, sari material, and bracelets. In the shop where fabric and saris were sold, the seated, barefoot shopkeeper threw bolts of material, which unrolled in front of us on a long platform. It made it easy to decide which pieces we wanted to buy.

Having walked enough, we took a taxi back to our hotel and got ready for dinner at the Rambagh Palace Hotel. Mother was treating. We all took showers. Mother wrote in her travel journal, "I showered cautiously—nervous that I might slip and fall in the wet bathroom. While showering, at least an inch of water covered the floor. There was a drain in the middle of the floor that slowly let the water out."

After we dressed for the evening, she told the girls, "We are going to a fancy hotel for dinner. I don't want you to eat with your fingers."

Tara replied, "Okay. We'll use forks and spoons for everything."

As soon as everyone was ready, we took a taxi to the Rambagh Palace Hotel, which was much larger than I expected. The palatial architecture was impressive. The brightly lit dining room had about fifty people, a little less than half full. The guests appeared to be part of a tour group. In the middle of the room several sitar players were playing Indian music. I ordered mixed grill for all of us. Mother liked the vegetables but didn't care much for the tough goat meat. The rolls with the meal were excellent.

I was glad to see that the girls were not eating with their fingers. At one point, I looked over at Tara, who was cutting her roll into small pieces with a knife and fork. Then she used the fork to pick up the pieces and put them in her mouth. She was following Mother's instructions—to the letter. At the end of the meal, we all loved our dessert of chocolate cake and ice cream.

The next day, we took another bus tour. Our bus dropped us off at the base of a mountain. From this point, we rode on an elephant to visit a fort and a winter palace. To get on the elephant, we climbed up a ladder and then stepped into a small tent-like arrangement with a canopy roof. There was space for about six people. The trip up the mountain took about an hour on the swaying elephant.

We passed at least five foreign tour groups on elephants. One group appeared to be from Russia. On our return, the ladder was not ready for us—which was typical of how arrangements proceeded (or lagged!) in India. We had to wait while the turbaned elephant handler called for a young man to bring the ladder, so we could climb down to the ground.

Back on the bus, the tour guide was extremely pleasant, which added to the trip. I think he was so friendly with us because of how interested Tara and Rita were in everything they saw. People on the trip were amazed at how well the girls spoke Hindi. To outsiders, our family group appeared to be Americans visiting India.

The following day, we went to the bus terminal to catch the deluxe bus back to Delhi. When I showed the driver our tickets, he said that they were one-way tickets. We started having a loud discussion in Hindi, because I thought Madhu had bought roundtrip bus tickets. The driver convinced me that I was wrong, and I paid him for our tickets.

I noticed that Mother was covering her ears and looked upset. I explained the problem to her. She said, "If I had known this, I would have insisted that we fly back to Delhi."

The long ride back was bumpy and uncomfortable. At times, it was scary due to the driver's speed and near collisions as we passed other vehicles. Mother said, "It feels like the driver is driving on the wrong side of the road, even though I know he isn't. I wish he'd drive slower."

We made it back safely to the Gupta family home at 10:30 p.m. Dinner was waiting for us. We were embarrassed and apologized that we were so late. As usual, we heard, "No problem, no problem." Immediately after dinner, we went upstairs to bed—exhausted by the trip.

Delhi to Chamba via Pathankot

After our sightseeing trips to Agra and Jaipur and our Delhi shopping and sightseeing, we were scheduled to leave for Pathankot by an evening train and then by jeep to our government quarters at Chamba. Sherri, the daughter of a good friend, planned to travel with us. She arrived at Gupta's house an hour before we needed to depart, wearing a fashionable woolen coat. Her long black hair was in a braid down to her waist. She was fourteen but looked eighteen. After being introduced, she said in perfect English. "It's a pleasure to meet you, Mrs. Griscom. You have a lovely daughter and grandchildren."

Mother replied. "Thanks. Where do you go to school?"

Sherri answered. "I go to a boarding school in Dalhousie. It's just two hours from Chamba, where my dad is Deputy Commissioner."

Mother quickly connected with Sherri's warm personality and was glad to have her travelling with us.

I engaged a taxi to take us to the railway station. Steve had taken some of our bags when he went to Pathankot, but still it was a miracle that we were able to get all our luggage in the taxi and on the rooftop carrier. While driving to the station, Mother mentioned, "I like how the driver is driving so slowly."

I said. "He has to because he keeps checking a suitcase on the top of the taxi with one of his hands."

"Do you think this is safe?"

"It's fine."

At the train station, the huge crowds of people amazed Mother. As soon as we got out of our taxi, we were surrounded by coolies shouting at us.

Tara said. "Grandmother, they think that we are foreigners so they can overcharge us."

I started talking with them in Hindi, and many of the coolies disappeared, realizing that we were not typical tourists. I hired two coolies to carry the larger pieces of luggage, and we carried the smaller bags. The five of us and the two coolies started out. It was a long walk up and down stairs to the train platform. When we finally got to our waiting train, one of the coolies was missing. The one with us unloaded the luggage from the top of his head and went to look for the other one.

Soon he came back with the second coolie, who demanded in Hindi, "Give us one hundred rupees."[31]

Tara, Rita, and I started arguing loudly about the price. Mother covered her ears, as she often did when there was too much loud talk in Hindi. I lowered my voice and explained that he was asking an exorbitant amount for the work. Finally, a lower price was settled.

We boarded the train and went into our reserved sleeping compartment. Sitting on the lower sleeping berth was a foreign woman. I politely told her, "This compartment is reserved for our family."

She replied, "I was advised to arrive at the station early, find an empty compartment, and wait there for the conductor." Then she told us about herself. "I am French by birth and a Hindu devotee. I am on a religious pilgrimage to Vaishna Devi in Jammu."

When the conductor came to check our tickets, he said that he would throw the lady out of our compartment. We felt that she had been given misinformation, so we decided to let her stay.

When our pilgrim went out to smoke in the hallway, we packed our money and passports in Sherri's metal trunk and locked it for safety's sake. Tara, Rita, Sherri, and I opened our bedroll and made the beds. We all climbed into our narrow sleeping berths. Our pilgrim returned, spread out a well-used sleeping bag on the floor, and laid down. In a few minutes, she was snoring loudly.

We got up at six, an hour before our scheduled morning arrival time, and took turns going to the bathroom. As we folded up the bedding, the conductor shouted, "About to arrive at Pathankot."

This was fifteen minutes ahead of schedule. We quickly packed all

---

[31] Three dollars

Delhi to Chamba via Pathankot

our things and woke our pilgrim, who went to the bathroom. When she returned, she was followed by the conductor, who announced, "We are at Pathankot. Everyone needs to get off the train."

We struggled with our luggage and left the compartment. Our pilgrim got out last and started putting on the rest of her clothes while standing on the station platform. She wore the rattiest-looking fur jacket that Mother and I had ever seen. As she walked off, we all said our *goodbyes*.

Two coolies rushed up to us, and I hired them. We started walking to the waiting room. Halfway there, we met Steve. He looked very nice, in a long, woolen topcoat, and he took us to the government forestry jeep, and a second one, which was on loan. There were six of us plus two drivers and a servant who had come from Chamba with our jeep driver. The second driver was from Pathankot. I introduced Mother to Steve's driver, Prakash, who wore Western clothes—except for a plaid scarf wrapped around his neck and over his head Indian-style. From the train station, Prakash took us to the home of Gurdeep Singh and Mrs. Singh, our good friends.

Gurdeep Singh was a forest contractor. His family business bought standing timber from the Himachal and Jammu Kashmir governments for sale throughout India. Much of his work was in the forests of Chamba and Jammu. Our short stay in Pathankot with the Singh family was a refreshing break after the overnight train trip.

Gurdeep and his wife welcomed us to their home. He was wearing a bathrobe, and she wore woolen slacks and a sweater that looked like it came from the United States. Gurdeep's parents also lived with them. His father was active in the business at Pathankot but didn't go out into the forests. He spoke to Mother in English and showed her the timber stacked at the side of their house, ready for sale. Then he introduced her to his wife, who didn't speak English. Tara and Rita served as translators when Mother talked with her.

Next, we were taken upstairs to a bedroom with a king-size bed. The room faced an open, flat-roof patio with lawn chairs on it. There was a connecting bedroom and bathroom. We were urged to take showers, which Sherrie and I did. Tara and Rita played outside on the patio.

In about forty-five minutes, we were called to breakfast. Gurdeep had changed and was now wearing woolen pants, a V-neck sweater, a huge purple turban, and a tie to match. His father was wearing a white turban. Breakfast consisted of juice, corn flakes, hot milk, lamb chops covered with peas, soft-boiled eggs, and toast served on American Corningware. We had a choice of coffee or tea.

While we were eating, a bird flew into the room and landed on the fan directly over the table. Mother was startled and jumped up from her seat.

Gurdeep's father asked, "Did he make a mess in your food?"

"No, everything's fine."

I think the bird was building a nest in the fan, because a tiny branch fell on the table near me.

After breakfast, we sat in their sunny garden. The Singhs had a little girl about eighteen months old named Goodiya. Her long, black, braided hair was laced with pink ribbons. She was friendly with Mother, which surprised me since Tara and Rita had been shy with their grandmother when they first met.

The family sat in the warm sun with us. We talked a lot about life in India and America. Goodiya's two older sisters were away at a Dehradun boarding school. Gurdeep had gone to college in Chicago. His father had a brother, who was a doctor on Long Island.

During one of our discussions, Gurdeep said to Mother, "What are your thoughts about Watergate and President Nixon?"

She replied, "We don't talk about him."

Then everyone broke into peals of laughter.

After our short stay at Gurdeep's home, we started the last leg of our journey, which was supposed to take four hours. On our way out of town, we stopped to buy fresh vegetables, fruits, and household supplies. As we left the plains, we began a gentle climb into the mountains. We went through primitive, small villages. At one village, where we stopped for a few minutes, the villagers were wearing torn, dull-colored clothes. We started back on our journey, and the road became steeper. The highest point on the trip was 8,000 feet above sea level. Sometimes, we passed herds of sheep and goats traveling on the road. In many places, there were flat, terraced fields with stone walls along their outer edges.

Steve explained, "Step farming is necessary to prevent soil erosion and large landslides."

Soon after he mentioned this, we had to stop for a huge landslide that had blocked the road. Scantily dressed coolies were clearing the road with shovels and pick axes. They seemed to have a system for this: One coolie held a shovel, which had a rope attached to it. A second coolie held the rope and pulled the shovel, which was filled with rocks and mud. While we waited for the road to be cleared, we saw a group of men sitting on the ground playing cards as they waited for traffic to start up again. Once the road was cleared for single-lane traffic, we continued our journey.

Coolies clearing the landslide on the road to Chamba

Halfway to Chamba, we saw a mountain spring, and the girls asked to stop for a drink. I felt that this clear, fast-flowing water was safe for them to drink. After gulping down some water, Tara and Rita started to chase each other.

Travelers on the road to Chamba playing cards while landslide is cleared

Steve shouted. "That's enough! No more running."

Today they obeyed, although they weren't always so good about following instructions. With Grandmother watching them, they were on their best behavior.

We all got back in the jeep. Prakash watchfully checked to see that no one got their fingers caught when he shut the doors. He drove carefully on the hairpin curves and narrow roads. At every curve, he blew his horn to warn approaching vehicles that we were coming. Sometimes, the buses and trucks coming from the other direction were partially on our side of the road.

Mother asked. "How much help will the low, stone guard rails be if a truck rams into us?"

I admitted, "Probably not much help. If the jeep goes off the road here, it will tumble down a thousand feet."

Mother said, "Prakash must have nerves of steel to drive on these mountain roads. He is a skillful driver, but the roads make me nervous."

As we got close to Chamba, we went across a bridge. It was just wide enough for one vehicle to cross. Mother said. "This is the oldest suspension bridge I have ever seen."

Soon after the bridge, we drove into the forest rest house compound, piled out of the jeep, and went through a gate in a wooden fence with crisscrossed boards. Finally, we were at our two-story, Chamba home.

Suspension bridge just before the town of Chamba

22

Mother's Stay at Chamba

After a week of nonstop activities in Delhi, Agra, and Jaipur, it felt good to be back home at Chamba. I led Mother up the steps to the front door. She remarked. "I like your large, fenced-in front yard."

We entered the house, which felt cold after the sunny front yard. We went into our spacious living room, where there was an electric space heater and an *angithi*, a small metal box with burning charcoal.

Mother sitting in the front yard of our Chamba home

Mother looked at our fireplace, which had a large plastic screen with a hand-embroidered cloth piece mounted on it. She asked, "Why don't you use the fireplace?"

I said. "We keep the chimney covered to prevent rodents from coming into the house."

Man Singh, our private servant, brought us tea. He was a young teenager and worked for us in hopes of getting a government job. Since Madhu was in charge of hiring some of the office staff in his jurisdiction, he was able to hire our personal servants when they became eighteen and were suitable for the job. Sometimes he asked a colleague to do this for him.

The phone started ringing. Friends were calling to invite us for lunches and dinners to meet Mother. One call was from Tilak *Mama* (Uncle). He said that he was sending us dinner. I thanked him.

Then I showed Mother around the house. She was surprised to find that a refrigerator in the dining room was turned off. We didn't use it in the winter since the house wasn't heated and food stayed cold. The kitchen had a two-burner gas stove, a kerosene stove, and a small oven. All the walls of the house were cement and were freshly white-washed. On the second story, there were three bedrooms, two bathrooms, and an open porch that faced the front yard.

After I settled Mother in her bedroom, I showed her how things worked in the bathroom. There was wooden stool for her to sit on while she took her Indian bucket shower and an electric heating rod for heating the water that she had to be careful about. I suggested that she call me to heat the water for her shower. Mother unpacked her suitcases and had a quick nap while I checked about her dinner. Tilak Mama was bringing Indian food for us, but I needed to make some American food for Mother. I boiled fresh cauliflower and gave Man Singh the ingredients for vegetable soup. He started the soup, and I went upstairs to unpack my own things. Tara and Rita went to their rooms to put away the clothes, toys, and other gifts from Grandmother.

A little later, Steve brought a cocktail up to Mother's room, along with one for himself. While talking with him, Mother said, "I think we should put a sign on my door that says *English Only in This Room.*"

Steve laughed and said, "Maybe we should start some Hindi lessons for you." He began with *Namaste*, explaining, "You should try saying *Namaste* when you greet people instead of *Hi*, especially with the servants."

For Mother's second day at Chamba, I had invited family and some close friends for afternoon tea. *Mami* (Aunt), Tilak Mama, and their

Mother's Stay at Chamba

two children—along with their dog, Tiger—were the first to arrive. Their daughter, Dipika, had just enrolled in high school at Chamba, and their son, Sanjeev, was in medical school at Shimla. Tilak Mama had been transferred to Chamba as transport manager two months back.

Mama's brownish-yellow-haired dog, Tiger, was a combination of Pekinese and Cocker Spaniel. He was on a leash, and we tied him to the back door. Tara and Rita told their grandmother about Tiger. Tara explained, "He sleeps in bed with Mama and Mami and is their hot water bottle."

Rita added. "He wears knitted boots in their bed so he doesn't get the sheets dirty."

Also at the afternoon tea were members of the Malhotra family. Dr. Hari Priya Malhotra, dressed in a purple sari, was one of my best friends. She was a lady doctor in the Chamba hospital. Her husband, Harish Malhotra, was an electrical engineer for the town. Their one-year-old son, Wrinku, was with them. Steve wanted to show them slides of our hiking trips when we were posted at Rohru, but the electricity kept going off. Harish made several phone calls to his office people. He was embarrassed and wanted them to get the electricity on as quickly as possible. Finally, the electricity came on, and we watched the slides.

Another set of guests was Mr. and Mrs. Vaidyanathan and their two children. Mr. Vaidyanathan was the Superintendent of Police. His wife had a vivacious face and beautiful teeth. She wore an embroidered, maroon sari. Their two-year-old daughter was dressed in their native dress from Madras, a long, embroidered, beaded dress. She looked like a little doll. Their son was about four. He wore a bright, checked outfit with the shirt down to his knees. Mother connected with Mrs. Vaidyanathan, who spoke English all the time.

After the guests left, Steve and Mother had drinks. Then we all went to the dining room. We sat at the dinner table and warmed our feet with the electric space heater and the charcoal heater, both of which were on the cold concrete floor. Dinner was baked, stuffed chicken, boiled peas, and mashed potatoes followed by a dessert of custard and fruit. I served Steve, Tara, Rita, Mother, and myself.

Mother said. "Just give me a little dessert, and if I like it, I'll ask for more." During her time with us, she was careful about what she ate and drank. Boiled water was a must, and she wanted no spices in her food.

During our dinner, we spent a lot of time talking about whether my dad could make a trip to India. Mother had come alone this time because she felt that Dad couldn't handle the trip. Now that she was here, she felt that he could have made the trip with some adjustments, and she wanted him to come on her next visit.[32]

Rajinder, Mother, Elma, Dad, Tara and Rita at Mandi

Madhu and Mother visiting a Chamba temple

[32] Mother and Dad did come together in 1981 when Madhu was posted a second time at Chamba. This was after Madhu was promoted to the position of Conservator.

Mother's Stay at Chamba

She suggested. "I think that if Dad comes, we should cut out the Agra and Jaipur part of the trip. The sightseeing was too hectic, and eating in different restaurants was risky."

Mother never liked the filth, poverty, and strange foods that she experienced during the sightseeing trips. The narrow mountain roads frightened her, and just as I had once experienced, she was overwhelmed by the constant talk in Hindi.

She looked quite proud as she added. "Elma has become immune to all of this."[33]

Mother and Elma on the road above Chamba

---

[33] Her exact notes from her journal were, "Elma is completely Indianized, but at times there is rebellion against it." I believe that the rebellion referred to my arguments with the coolies, who tried to overcharge us because we were foreigners.

23

Family Visit from Pennsylvania

Family visits from the United States were rare and memorable. I had lived in India for twenty-two years, and we now lived in Shimla. It was Madhu's seventh posting in the Forest Department, and the upcoming visit of Aunt Elma and Uncle Charles would be the sixth American family visit.

Elma was my father's only sister. She had a warm personality and infectious humor. It was her first visit to India, and it would be Charles's second visit. During World War II, he had been stationed at a United States Air Force Base in the village of Kharagpur near Calcutta in Eastern Bengal. I was surprised that Charles, who liked everything in perfect order, wanted to return to India, where things didn't always go as planned. Still, he was keen to visit us and hoped to make a trip to Calcutta to revive fond memories of weekends spent there with friends from his air force unit.

Preparation for their visit consisted of a thorough cleaning of our three-bedroom, government flat in the Khalini Forest Colony just below Cart Road, which circled the town of Shimla. We usually cooked Indian food, but during Elma's and Charles' stay we planned to cook American meals.

About a month back, they had asked us what to bring for themselves and what we wanted. They said that they would devote one large suitcase for our wish list. For themselves, we suggested that they bring summer and fall clothes, all their medications, and a few nonperishable food items, like their favorite cereals. Our list of gifts included many small items and one big one: a vacuum cleaner. We assured them that we didn't expect everything on the list, and suggested that they pick and choose what they were able to bring. We figured that they wouldn't bring the vacuum cleaner, but we kept it on the list.

Two days before their arrival, Rita, and I traveled in our Fiat by road from Shimla to Delhi to meet them at the Delhi International Airport. (Tara was still at her Chandigarh hostel; we had agreed to pick her up on our way home.) We were staying at the Himachal *Bhawan*, a guest house run by the Himachal government for its officers and their families. The guest house was near Connaught Circle, an established shopping center and office area of Delhi.

Delhi Arrival – May 1984

The evening of their arrival, we took a taxi to the airport and waited outside the arrival area. Rita, now fourteen, had lots of questions about her relatives, whom she hadn't seen since she and Tara visited the United States and attended fourth and sixth grades in Michigan for three months.

As we waited, I saw Elma and Charles walking towards us with two baggage carts piled high with luggage. We greeted each other with big hugs and headed to our taxi. We found the driver sleeping in the back seat. I woke him, and he loaded the four large suitcases, two good-sized handbags, a purse, a briefcase, and two umbrellas into the taxi. We reached the Himachal Bhawan and quickly settled Elma and Charles in their air-conditioned room.

Delhi Sightseeing

The next day, we caught an afternoon sightseeing bus at nearby Connaught Circle and listened intently to our driver as he described the Delhi landmarks. Aunt Elma was shocked by the many beggars and slum areas we passed along the way. Tent-like constructions with plastic or gunny-bag roofs were often located near a large hotel or a historic fort. The afternoon of sightseeing went well, but Elma and Charles were ready for bed as soon as we got back to the guest house.

Agra and the Taj Mahal

By eight the next morning, we were on our way to Agra—not too bad for two jetlagged American tourists and their Indian-American family. Our Ambassador taxi wasn't air-conditioned, so it was hot at first. Once we got going, it cooled down a little, but it heated up again towards noontime. Close to Agra, we heard a loud bang. We didn't know what had happened until Elma cried out. "Oh my goodness! Look at the front window."

We were shocked to see the shattered window.

Our driver slowed down and said. "A stone broke the window."

I said, "Where will you get it fixed?"

The conversation continued in Hindi.

"I will drive with the broken window and get it fixed at Agra while you are at the Taj Mahal."

"How far is Agra?"

"We are almost there."

The driver stopped and made a temporary arrangement to keep the glass from breaking more, and then we started out again. As the taxi sped up, pieces of glass flew out from the window. We asked the driver to slow down. All of us were nervous.

Finally, we reached Agra and the Taj Mahal. The driver asked us to give him half the payment for the trip, so he had cash for the repairs. We gave him the money, and he left. I thought, *Hopefully, he'll be back.*

We waited in a long line for our admission tickets, bought them, and entered the Taj Mahal area. The heat and exhaustion proved to be too much for our guests. Almost immediately, Elma said, "I need to sit down."

Taj Mahal

We saw some benches under the entrance roof and walked over to them. But before we got Elma seated, she folded up, fell to the ground, and passed out. We fanned her, and she came to. She whispered, "I'm okay."

We helped her up and gave her a Coke. After more fanning, she looked better. She wanted us to walk to the Taj and go inside the mausoleum without her. She said. "I'll be fine here in the shade."

At her insistence, we started off for the Taj and took pictures on the way. As always, I was amazed at the eye-catching beauty of the Taj Mahal, which I had taken guests to see on several other occasions. Charles was anxious to get back to Elma, so we went inside the mausoleum but didn't stop for explanations about the tombs and inlaid marble walls.

On our return, we found Elma talking to a tourist. Unsteadily, she got up and said, "I feel bad I missed the Taj, but there was no way I could have walked around in the scorching heat."

We left the Taj and found our taxi in a long line of taxis. Much to our relief, the front window glass had been replaced. We got into the taxi and headed for the five-star Mughal Sheraton Hotel for lunch. The air-conditioned dining room felt refreshing after the Agra heat. Our American lunch of sandwiches and soup was delicious. Feeling rejuvenated, we decided to visit the Tomb of Akbar the Great and possibly a fort. The visit to Akbar's Tomb went well.[34] We had a personable guide who spoke fluent English with an Indian accent. We admired the beauty of the white marble tomb.

The heat continued to bother Elma and Charles, who were in their sixties, so after the tomb visit, we headed back to Delhi. The Sikh taxi driver drove too fast, passing one car after another. When we asked him to slow down, he complied for about five minutes and then started speeding again.

Back at the Himachal Bhawan, we went to our rooms for a short rest before a late dinner. We got a call from Elma saying that Charles was not feeling well. We rushed over to their room and found that he was feeling dizzy and unable to get out of bed. He said, "I need to see a doctor. I'm not sure what's wrong, but it's not good."

We called the front desk, and they said that there was a doctor on call.

In a few minutes the clerk called and said, "The doctor will be here in thirty minutes."

Elma couldn't believe this. She compared the situation to the United States, where house calls by doctors were extremely rare. Even I was surprised. Home visits happened in the smaller towns of Himachal, where you often had a doctor friend, but we were in the capital of India.

In twenty minutes the doctor was in the room examining Charles. He took his blood pressure, checked his temperature, listened to his heart, and asked many questions. He was very personable, and during the examination we learned that his son was a doctor in Los Angeles. Our Delhi doctor suggested having boiled water, drinking lots of liquids, taking some medicine he was prescribing, and avoiding sightsee-

---

[34] The third Mughal Emperor, Akbar the Great (1555–1605), began the construction of his own tomb around 1600. After his death, his son Jahangir completed the construction in 1605-1613. Akbar was one of the greatest emperors in the history of India.

ing for at least one day. He said that Charles had heat exhaustion and was dehydrated.

We sent a hotel worker to a nearby pharmacy with the doctor's prescription and waited for the medicine. Our hotel doctor talked about his son in California, and we suggested that he might also go there to work. He said. "No thank you. I don't need to run numerous tests to make a diagnosis. I use tests when needed, but not for every little ailment. A good doctor in India uses his training, brain, and experience to diagnose, whereas this isn't possible in the United States. I like Delhi."

We got his point, agreed that he was happier here, and respected his opinion that visiting the United States was enough. The medicine arrived, which cost one hundred and fifty rupees,[35] and Charles took his first pill. Already he appeared on the road to recovery just from the comforting bedside manner of the guest house doctor.

Chandigarh

The next day, Charles was well enough for us to drive to Chandigarh, a five-hour drive in our white Fiat car. I was one of the few women driving in India at the time. When I had gotten my license in Chamba five years back, I was the first woman to get a driver's license in the district. We packed some luggage in the car and sent the rest to Shimla with a family friend.

The ride to Chandigarh involved following the Grand Trunk Highway. The highway shifted back and forth from a six-lane divided highway to four lanes with no central median. At times a car passed from the other direction, which placed it in our lane, traveling straight towards us. It was nerve racking. Speeds averaged about forty miles per hour.

Tara and Elma in front of her dorm in Chandigarh

We reached Chandigarh and went straight to the Government College for Women, where Tara was a pre-engineering student, the equivalent to twelfth grade in America. Madhu had come from Shimla in his government car with his driver and met us at Tara's dormitory. We were picking her up to

---

[35] Seven dollars

Family Visit from Pennsylvania

take her to Shimla, but first we had to drop her fan and a trunk at the home of her local guardians, who were friends from our Kulu and Chamba postings in the 1970s. Tara was friendly with their daughter Geetha and would return to Chandigarh for her final exams at the end of June.

Tara was excited to see us and showed Aunt Elma and Uncle Charles around her dorm. We met a couple of Tara's friends. They were respectful and conversed with us, even though they were busy lugging their possessions down to waiting cars and jeeps.

Madhu's driver helped us transport Tara's belongings to her local guardians' home. While there, Radhakrishan and his wife served us coffee accompanied by sandwiches and South Indian snacks which included *dosa* (a fermented type of crepe stuffed with potatoes) and *upama* (a cream of wheat dish with vegetables). Elma complimented Mrs. Radhakrishan on her green, plaid sari and asked how she did her kitchen work while wearing a sari. Mrs. Radhakrishan said, "No problem."

The conversation was in English, so Elma and Charles didn't have to guess what was being said. We discussed our plans to visit some of the Chandigarh attractions: Sukhna Lake, Rose Garden, and Nek Chand's Rock Garden, where rocks were displayed in every conceivable way. Chandigarh was hot but nothing like Delhi.

When sightseeing was complete, we left for Shimla. Elma and Charles decided to ride with me rather than in Steve's car because I drove at a sensible speed. The ride to Shimla began in the plains. We stopped at Parwanu for lunch at Timber Trail, a government-run restaurant. Charles enjoyed his lunch after we assured him that the food was safe to eat.

After we left the restaurant, we started up the steep, narrow road to Shimla. Usually there was a guard rail on the side of the road, but where there was no rail, the drop from the outer side of the road was quite scary. While negotiating hairpin curves, we often met another car, bus, truck, bicyclist, or an animal on our side of the road. Constantly, I had to be ready for the unexpected.

Each time we approached a curve, Rita called out. "Mom, blow the horn." Horn-blowing was a good way of warning oncoming traffic on these curvy roads.

We reached Shimla early that evening and drove into the parking area in front of our Khalini apartment. We stepped out of the car and immediately felt a refreshing, cool breeze.

Shimla Arrival

The first thing Elma said was, "What a difference! It was so hot in Delhi. These mountain views are stunning. What a welcome relief after that drive. Talk about harrowing!"

It was late afternoon. Steve had arrived before us and was standing in the parking area between the two apartment buildings. One two-story building had eight apartments, and it faced six larger apartments in a second two-story building. Our apartment was on the side which had eight apartments and was on the second floor. Steve greeted us and said, "Don't worry about the luggage. Our servants will bring things upstairs."

As we watched our bags being unloaded, Rita told Elma and Charles that the parking area between the two buildings was often used for badminton games during the daytime, when the forest officers took their vehicles to the office or went out on official tours. The parking lot had a wooden fence at one end where you could stand and look down the mountain, quite a commanding view.

Rita and Aunt Elma beside our Fiat at Kasumpti (Shimla)

Our living room at Kasumpti

After all the luggage was unloaded from the car, we picked up our small bags. Again, Steve insisted that we didn't need to worry about the luggage. He led Elma and Charles up to our second-floor apartment, and we went into the living room. A servant served us tea. The living room had a cement floor, a red Tibetan carpet, and a black, simulated-leather sofa with matching chairs. One wall had a set of windows that faced away from the parking lot and had a commanding view of the mountainside. The windows were open, and a cool breeze floated into the room.

After our tea, Aunt Elma asked to use the bathroom. I explained, "We have only one bathroom with a toilet. The second bathroom has a shower and is also used as the laundry room. We all share the bathrooms."

Then Elma said that she and Charles were tired, so I showed them their bedroom. I went into the kitchen to check about food. Our teenaged servant, Raj Kumar, had cooked dinner for us, which we would eat later that evening. We didn't usually have dinner until eight in the evening.

When Elma and Charles woke up, I offered them tea again. Having tea in the late afternoon was an Indian custom adopted from the British. As we drank our tea, I told them that our servant had already cooked an Indian meal for dinner, but I was making cheese and tomato sandwiches for them.

Elma and Charles went back into the bedroom and started bringing out the gifts they had brought for the family. We couldn't believe that they had actually managed to bring the requested vacuum cleaner all the way from the United States. Both Steve and I kept thanking them for the Hoover upright vacuum.

Shimla Mall

The morning of their second day at Shimla was low-key. Charles and Elma, wearing their bathrobes and sweatpants, watched the family activities. Elma remarked, "Everyone is very particular about their clothes. Steve dresses for the office as though he is going to Madison Avenue. It seems like your iron is always on."

I was busy supervising a part-time servant, who was cleaning the apartment and washing the dirty clothes from our trip. Many of the clothes were hand-washed, but some were washed in a simplistic washing machine. After the clothes were washed, they were hung outside on a line stretched across the front of the apartment. To do this, the servant had to lean out of an open window to hang clothes on the clothesline, which was just below the windowsill.

After lunch and a short nap, we all got into the car and were off to the Shimla Mall. It was a steep climb from Khalini. When we got close to the Mall Road, we left our car in a small parking lot for Clarkes Hotel, and then we started walking up to the Mall Road. Since the time when Shimla was the British summer capital, the Mall Road was reserved for pedestrians. Only ambulances, fire trucks, the governor's car, and ministers' cars were allowed to drive on the Mall Road.

Shimla Mall Road

While walking, we saw many others out for their afternoon walk. I greeted friends on the way. Some stopped to talk, and I introduced my American family from Pennsylvania.

Once we reached Scandal Point, we met Steve's sister Vidya and her husband Chauhan. Both had government jobs in the Mandi District Welfare Department. They were on tour to Shimla and were staying at Chauhan's flat in San Joli, Shimla. We had coffee with them at the Indian Coffee House. While there, they invited us to Chauhan's son's wedding, which was being held in a village near Kotkhai, where they had their apple orchard. Chauhan said. "An Indian village wedding would be something new and different for you. I hope all of you can come."

Aunt Elma replied, "I'd love to come if Elma can make the arrangements for us."

We left the restaurant and continued our walk on the Mall. We reached a lovely, old, stone church on the Ridge and took a quick look. I said that we would save our visit to

Steps leading to Middle Bazaar

Family Visit from Pennsylvania

the church for another trip. Lights were now visible, and the Mall was gorgeous with no vehicles and many brightly dressed walkers. May and June were the peak months for tourists to visit Shimla. Less than half the people we saw were year-round residents. It was getting late now, so we started walking down the hill to our car and returned to Khalini.

Shopping at Subzi Mandi (Vegetable Market)

Our private servant, Raj Kumar, did most of the Indian cooking, and I made the American food. I kept trying to find dishes that my American family could eat. Elma told me. "You don't have to go to so much trouble."

I said. "No big deal."

We sat together and figured out some American meals. Then I made a shopping list and suggested. "Let's all go shopping at *subzi mandi*. It's the main vegetable, fruit, ration, and meat market."

We all got into a jeep with four-wheel drive and headed up to Cart Road, the main road, which circled below and around the whole town of Shimla. Then we turned up a narrow road, which went straight uphill. A car approached us from above and stopped at a slightly wider section of the road, so we were able to go by it without having to stop in the middle of that hill.

"Thank goodness!" Elma declared.

We eventually reached a parking lot, where we left the jeep and had a short, level walk to the shops. We passed a few vegetable stalls located on the ground along the footpath. Many of the shopkeepers called out in Hindi, "Fresh vegetables, very cheap, buy from us." After these stalls, we entered a large building that looked like an old stable and was filled with many open shops. This high-ceilinged building was my favorite place to buy vegetables. The shopkeepers called out to me, *"Namaste, meme sahib."* (Greetings, respected woman.)

I replied back in a friendly tone. We looked at beans, cauliflower, tomatoes, peas, okra, bananas, and peaches. I picked out the freshest ones. I asked Elma if there was anything she'd like to try.

She said, "The okra looks good and is something that we don't often get in our American supermarkets."

The *subzi wala* (shopkeeper) weighed the vegetables, and I bargained with him about the prices. After I paid him, Raj Kumar put our purchases in the bags we had brought with us and carried them back to the jeep.

As we walked along the road and looked into the shops, Elma asked if there were canned vegetables in any of the stores. I told her that there were, but they were expensive and not that great.

The market was full of Indian shoppers, and we were the only foreigners. Porters were carrying large bags on their backs. I told Elma and Charles that trucks brought rations and supplies up the hill to the parking lot where we had left our jeep, and from there the porters or coolies carried everything to the shops. Many of the coolies were *Ghorkhas*, Nepalis. We returned to our jeep, and I sent Raj Kumar to get chicken.

Elma asked. "Why didn't we go with him?"

I hesitated. Then I said, "I was afraid you wouldn't like the looks of the meat market. Some of the meat is lying unrefrigerated on low tables, and whole animals are hanging on poles, with flies sitting on the meat."

Elma reminded me. "Don't forget that my father owned a butcher shop, and I often visited his shop."

Prep for Kotkhai/Kari Wedding

We planned to attend the village wedding of Chauhan's son at his ancestral family home, which was not accessible by road. The marriage was being held at the orchard because Chauhan's sons lived in the village of Kari, where they managed the apple orchard. We wanted to make sure that Elma would be able to handle the steep hike up to Kari village. To strengthen her hiking abilities, we suggested that she walk up from Cart Road to the Mall Road instead of taking the car. Walking at the height of 6,000 feet was tough for her, especially when she wasn't used to walking much at all. Still, she wanted to be able to make the climb for the wedding, so she agreed to test herself to see if she could do the extra walking to get in shape.

Kari Village Wedding

We were off to the Chauhan wedding. Steve and the girls left first, because he had some forestry work to do on the way. Then Elma, Charles, Raj Kumar, and I got into our Fiat. I drove very carefully along the treacherous road, which had lots of blind curves. I realized how much I missed Rita's reminders to blow my horn as I rounded the curves.

There were sheer drops along the outer edge of the road, which was quite bumpy, even though it was paved. We didn't stop until we reached the Kotkhai Rest House, where we met up with Tara, Rita, Steve, and his forest department staff members.

Family Visit from Pennsylvania

After a cup of tea and light snacks, we started out in the cars for a short distance. Then we got out and began our walk up the steep mountain trail. It was about a one mile climb, but it seemed like more because of the 6,000 to 7,000 feet altitude. The views of heavily forested mountains and green valleys were breathtaking.

Elma stopped every fifteen minutes, because she felt out of breath. She said, "If I had known how tough the climb was, I might not have attempted it."

The rest of the group didn't mind the hike and the altitude.

At the end of our one hour climb, we reached a large open compound, which was where the wedding was being held. The compound surrounded Chauhan's spacious orchard home. Charles and Elma were surprised by the huge crowd of people. It looked like five hundred guests. We were greeted by Steve's sister Vidya and her husband Chauhan, who led us into a dining area crowded with guests. Some of Steve's family worked their way over to greet us. Tea and hors d'oeuvres were served, but according to instructions, Elma and Charles said, "No thank you." I knew they felt rude about refusing food, so I assured them that the family understood that they weren't used to the spicy food. Also, I was a little concerned that they might pick up an infection.

We sat down and surveyed the scene. Guests dressed in their bright Indian wedding finery were milling around, drinking tea, and eating snacks. Soon, Chauhan ushered us to a verandah that overlooked an open, grassy area, where the bride, groom, and other guests were dancing. Chauhan sent a young man to get us chairs. We felt like VIP guests. Steve and I went to a large tent for food, while Tara, Rita, Charles, and Elma stayed on the verandah and ate the food that we had brought from home.

Charles used his tape recorder to tape descriptions of the activities with the music playing in the background. Several small bands were playing Indian songs. Some guests danced with partners, and others danced in small groups. Tara and Rita joined the dancers and were experts. Charles took pictures, along with two professional photographers. The dancing, music, and festivities at this village mountain wedding were amazing scenes. Elma said, "I've never seen a wedding like this before. Charles and I will never forget it."

At five in the afternoon, we started down the mountain to our cars. The long ride home was quite dark except for occasional lightning flashes and the headlights of a few oncoming cars.

St. Bede's College

Two days later, we drove to St. Bede's Women's College and School, which was run by nuns. It was located below Cart Road on the side of the mountain that had few buildings but many large deodar trees and smaller pine trees. The old stone college buildings were charming. Some had been built in the 1860s. Rita was to start eleventh standard at St. Bede's in June.[36]

We got out and walked around the cool, shady area. Young women were moving from class to class. There were a few male lecturers and other male staff, but most of the faculty and non-teaching staff were women. Some classes were taught by nuns, but most were taught by Indians living in Shimla with degrees from various Indian colleges.

We walked up to a lovely old stone church and hoped to go inside. It was closed, but there was a sign on the door: *Open for church services on Sunday.* Elma asked. "Do you think we could attend the Sunday service?"

I said. "I've never been to a church service here, but I would love to go with you and Uncle Charles."

Visit to Anjana's Home in Kasumpti

Madhu's sister Anjana asked us for tea to meet with relatives. She lived in a section of Shimla called Kasumpti, which was about two miles from our apartment. We travelled by car on a narrow, curvy, hilly road and passed through Kasumpti bazaar, which seemed like a small town compared to the Mall Road bazaar.

From the bazaar our car climbed a steep hill, and we drove into a parking lot. We got out of our car and climbed up three flights of stairs to Anjana's apartment on the top floor. We entered the apartment through a narrow hallway into the drawing room, where we were greeted by Anjana's husband, Madhu's sister Hansa, her family, Anjana's daughter Minu, her husband, and their young son.

After the customary *Namaste* greetings, everyone asked Elma and Charles. "How are you liking Shimla?"

Then Hansa's husband, Suresh, moved next to Charles and Elma and started a conversation about Hindu religion.

In a previous conversation at our home, Suresh had outlined three basic precepts when talking with Elma and Charles:

---

[36] Eleventh and twelfth standards (grades) took place either in high school or in college. Rita chose to attend college for these two years.

1. Incarnation
2. God in everything
3. Caste system – much misunderstood
    Brahman – head, priests, pandits
    Kshatriya – businessmen, merchants
    Rajput – warriors
    Scheduled caste – menial job workers

Continuing with the earlier conversation, Suresh said. "All castes are equal and have their jobs."

Suresh was very articulate. Also, he explained about the many gods. "All the gods are a means of helping an individual be one with God." He added that in religion there were many paths, many sticks[37] to help people make it to the top.

Suresh had a lot of knowledge about Christianity. Aunt Elma later told me that she thought he sounded like a born-again Christian. He and his family were very spiritual, especially his son Raman, unlike Steve and I who were pretty casual in our outlooks about religion. While waiting for tea, Suresh was teaching Anjana's grandson Sonu to say, *"Subha pyar karo, dupher pyar karo, sham pyar karo."* (Love in the morning, love in the daytime, love at night—the way to God.)

Suresh added. "The heart of the matter is that God is love, and God is in everything that lives."

We had tea, talked a lot, and then returned home.

St. Bede's Church and Mother's Day

On Sunday, we attended a Mother's Day service at St. Bede's Church. Most of the people there were students from the boarding school and college. The theme of the sermon was, "Don't be discouraged or feel you can't do anything." The priest told a story of two frogs on a world tour, who fell into cream. One gave up and drowned, while the other swam, churned around, and made butter that supported him.

On the way home, Elma remarked. "The sermon was for the young, Indian, female students, but it would be appropriate for our church at home. I hope Rita, Tara, and the girls in the church took the message to heart."

Later in the day we were having guests for tea, so after the service we looked through my cookbook and index cards for ideas. One of the

---

[37] I think Suresh meant that the sticks pointed people in the right direction.

recipes we chose was a chocolate cake. We made it from scratch—no cake mixes in India.

After the tea, we left for our Mother's Day dinner at the Oberoi Hotel, which was called Clarkes. We rode up in the car to the hotel parking lot and then walked the rest of the way. There was a gorgeous full moon.

We had chosen Clarkes for dinner, because they served American food. Also, Steve's nephew worked there and was able to get a discount for our meal. We had baked fish for dinner that tasted like it was made from an American recipe. Charles had his favorite Bloody Mary. It was an evening of fine dining and excellent company.

After Elma's and Charles' visit to Shimla, we traveled to Calcutta, Darjeeling, and back to Delhi before they left for the United States. It would be years before I would see them again, and I missed their company dearly.

part iv
Amalgamation

24

Surprising Comments by Friends

In the spring of 1980 while posted at Chamba, Madhu went on a government tour to Shimla. I accompanied him. Both Tara and Rita were in boarding school at the Sacred Heart Convent School in Dalhousie. While at Shimla, Madhu and I attended a dinner party hosted by some of our Indian friends. As usual, the men and women sat in two separate groups in the large, high-ceilinged living room. The men drank their favorite brands of Indian liquor and talked loudly. The women had juice, soda, or tea. They wore bright party saris or a *salwar kameez* and talked animatedly.

I listened attentively to the women's discussions in Hindi. Having lived eighteen years in India, I understood and spoke the language. The topic was about their unmarried sons, who were in the United States studying for graduate degrees or working for American companies.

At first, the talk was about where the young men were and what they were doing. One was at M.I.T., another at Stanford, and the rest scattered around the country in different colleges and workplaces.

Then my women friends began to discuss their thoughts on marriages for their sons. One woman friend voiced her fear. "I'm so afraid that my son who is working in Boston will marry an American woman."

Others agreed that they had the same worry.

I was amazed that they all talked so freely about their dislike of Indian-American marriages while I was listening to their discussions.

Surprising Comments by Friends

What did they think my marriage was? For a while, I simply bit my tongue and listened.

My friend from Chamba, who was wearing a peacock-colored sari added. "I don't want my son to marry an American so I keep trying to arrange his marriage with an Indian woman. The last time he visited, I introduced him to several well-educated, fair-complexioned women."

I asked. "What happened?"

She said. "He wasn't ready to make a commitment."

A short-haired, attractive woman from Shimla said. "I keep trying to fix my son up with Indian women in the United States. He's met a few but has shown no interest. I pray he doesn't marry an American."

At that point, I couldn't keep quiet any longer. I said. "How can you be so critical of Indian-American marriages in front of me?"

A close friend said. *"Aap Hindustanti hain."* ("You are an Indian.")

I quickly realized that she felt I was fully adjusted to Indian culture—that I was one of them. Indirectly, she was complimenting me on my biculturalism and my successful transition from the American way of life to the Indian way of life. After eighteen years of living in India, I felt comfortable with the Hindi language, relished Indian food, wore Indian clothes, socialized with Indians, ran a small carpet business, studied at Himachal colleges, accompanied my husband on forestry tours, worked as a teacher, and raised two daughters. Indeed, *"Aap Hindustanti hain"* was true.

25

Nomination or Not

Why had I come to Delhi in this sweltering heat? Angst had brought me here. My daughter Tara's entire future was uncertain because of the continued Hindu-Sikh conflicts and escalating violence in Punjab, which had halted the college entrance exams. So here I was in June of 1984 at the office of the Indian Nomination Board for admission to Indian engineering and medical colleges, trying to sort things out.

Delhi buildings

I had avoided the trip as long as I could. However, Tara's dream of getting admission to an Indian engineering college hinged on scoring well on the exams. Admission was very competitive. She had studied hard, taken extra tutoring classes, and scored first division in her previous exams. But the latest round of exams, which were to take place in Chandigarh, had been postponed due to the Punjab crisis, and she was still at our home in Shimla, waiting for the exams to be rescheduled.

The thought of dealing with Indian bureaucracy was unnerving. I had done it on earlier occasions, and it was always a challenge. At one point while trying to get some bank transactions done for my carpet export business, a bank officer had frankly told me. "You don't get your work done because you don't use bribery." Yet after twenty-two years of living in India, I still was unwilling to use bribery to get things done. You'd think I'd have learned by now.

I entered the sparsely furnished waiting room of the Nomination Board and approached a clerk, who was looking through a manila file folder on his desk. He asked me why I was here. I explained that my daughter Tara was an American citizen and studying at Government College for Women in Chandigarh. Her pre-engineering exams had been postponed indefinitely. I wanted to apply for her nomination as a foreign student to an Indian engineering college because of this uncertainty.

The clerk half-listened to me while he continued to go through his file folder. Then he got up, looked in the office behind his desk, and said, "You can go in now."

I was surprised to be shown into an official's inner office so quickly. I thought that I might have to beg or use bribery to see the officer. A tall, well-dressed man stood up and greeted me in English. I explained Tara's problem in detail and added that I was an American citizen married to an Indian national who was a Himachal Pradesh Forest Officer presently posted at Shimla.

Then in a shaky voice, I requested. "I am here to apply for my daughter Tara's nomination to an Indian engineering college. Please let me know what needs to be done."

After asking a few clarifying questions, which I quickly answered, the officer replied. "Your daughter doesn't have a chance of being nominated. First, most of the board seats are for foreign nationals from third-world countries. Second, we give a few seats to the children of Indian Foreign Service Officers who were born abroad and have foreign passports, but Tara doesn't fit this category. Third, without results from the pre-engineering exams, we can't nominate her."

I began my arguments in hopes of convincing him that Tara should be nominated. I said. "Postponement of her exams is out of our control. That's why I am here!"

I showed him how well she had done on last year's exams.

"I'm sorry, but we have to follow our rules. No pre-engineering exam results, no admission. Even if they have the exams in July or August, it won't do any good. By that time our list of nominees will be finalized."

"What about the Punjab colleges? They should take nominees from foreign students studying in Punjab who had to wait to take their exams."

"I'm sorry, but our list of nominees for these colleges are being finalized next week from our current candidates who have taken their exams."

I was very upset. I told him that my husband, Madhu, was an Indian national who studied abroad at Duke University. His education was funded by his parents and work study money from Duke. After getting two graduate degrees in forestry, he was one of the few Indian students who returned to their homeland to work. I argued. "I think his return warrants our daughter's admission in India."

Once I stopped talking, the official said. "If you want her admission so badly, why don't you change her citizenship to Indian nationality?"

At that point I was extremely frustrated. I realized that there was nothing more I could do. I could hear the dejection in my own voice as I said. "Thank you for your time. However, I don't plan to change her citizenship."

The officer replied. "I'll keep her paperwork, but frankly she has no chance as an American national."

I felt like crying as I left the office. Again, I had been unsuccessful in dealing with Indian authorities.

I climbed into a three-wheeler taxi for the ride back to my room at the Himachal Bhawan (guest house). I kept wondering, *Was bribery the solution to the nomination for Tara?* I hated

Delhi traffic

to think that the seemingly decent, straightforward officer would accept a bribe. In fact, I didn't even know how to offer a bribe, and I didn't feel that it was the right thing to do. Still, my mind kept reverting back to the office scene and thoughts of my disappointed family.

Why had I failed? What would Tara do now? Would her exams happen in the near future? Would the Punjab crisis be resolved? With all these questions running through my mind, I wanted to return home to my family at Shimla as quickly as possible.

Nomination or Not

I decided to spend the rest of the day at the Himachal Bhawan, and then take the night bus back to Shimla. However, when I reached the Bhawan, there was a lot of loud talk in the lobby. I asked. "What's all the commotion about?"

The reception clerk anxiously replied. "The Sikh Golden Temple in Amritsar was just attacked by Indian government troops. There are curfews in Amritsar and the rest of Punjab. Operation Blue Star is in full force."[38]

Learning this, I went up to my room to figure out what I should do next. My plan of taking the night bus to Shimla was uncertain because of the violent attack. That evening, I decided to chance it and went to the interstate bus terminal to see if the bus was operating. On the road to the terminal, there were many more police cars than usual. I saw policemen standing on the road with guns. The entire scene was eerie.

I was relieved to be able to reach the bus terminal safely. At the ticket window, I learned that the bus was going to Shimla, but the route was slightly changed to avoid entering the state of Punjab. I bought my ticket and boarded the bus. The whole trip was tense. On the way, policemen entered the bus, walked up and down the aisles with guns hanging from their shoulders, and questioned passengers. Twice, I was asked. "Are you a foreigner?" When I said that I was an American, they wanted to see my passport.

Finally, after a long night on the bus, I reached the Shimla bus terminal, where I was met by Tara and Madhu. On the car ride to our home, I tearfully explained the events of the office visit and the ride from Delhi to Shimla. Tara said. "Mom, I know you did your best."

Then Madhu added. "It looks like we'll have to look at our other option."

I knew he was thinking about Tara's admission to Grinnell College in Iowa. The previous week, she had received her acceptance to Grinnell's five-year program in which she could transfer to an engineering college after her third year. However, I was nervous about the idea of Tara going off to America on her own at age eighteen, especially to a world so different from the protected life of her Indian family, a convent boarding school, and a strict dorm in Chandigarh.

---

[38] Operation Blue Star was "an Indian military operation [that] occurred between 3–8 June 1984, ordered by Prime Minister Indira Gandhi in order to establish control over the Harmandir Sahib Complex in Amritsar, Punjab, and remove Jarnail Singh Bhindranwale and his armed followers from the complex buildings" (*http://en.wikipedia.org/wiki/Operation_Blue_Star*).

How did this finally play out? Tara accepted Grinnell's offer and began to prepare to leave for Iowa in mid-August. The postponed exams were rescheduled for mid-July, and we encouraged her to take them anyway. Grinnell said that they didn't need the exam results, but I wanted Tara to take the exams just in case things didn't work out in America. She had prepared for them and had time to take them before she left. It was better not to leave things unfinished.

Tara took her exams and completed them four days before her flight to the United States. In August of 1984, she left for a new and different life at Grinnell College.

26

My Own Return to College

My unfinished degree from Duke University was a thorn in my side. When both daughters were in school, I decided to go back to college.

In 1975, gaining admission to Himachal Pradesh University (HPU), an Indian state university, was a tedious process for a foreigner. Whenever I submitted one set of documents, they always seemed to ask for something else. For almost a year, I made many attempts and finally was accepted into BA Part II, which meant I had two years of classes and exams for my Bachelor of Arts degree. I had hoped to get into BA Part III, but that didn't happen.

One of my courses at HPU Chamba was Indian history, which I worried about passing. I read every assignment several times and got extra help from the professor. It paid off with a first division in the final exams and the highest marks in my class of young Indian students.

Mountainside view of Shimla

After completing my degree, I joined a master's correspondence program in English literature. This took another two years. I missed having professors to guide me and the company of other students. The program gave me the syllabus, names of books to read, and after that I was on my own to study for and appear in the semester exams.

After I completed my master's degree, Madhu was transferred to Shimla, and I got admission to a Master of Philosophy (MPhil) English Literature program at the head campus of HPU in Summerhill, Shimla. It was now 1985. Tara had left for Grinnell College in Iowa and Rita was a student in pre-university classes at St. Bede's College in Shimla.

I was excited about attending classes again. It was a four-mile trip from our Khalini government quarters to my MPhil classes at the university campus. In the morning I walked up Khalini Road, which was lined on both sides with deodar, oak, pine, and rhododendron trees. Once I reached Cart Road, I took a bus to the Summerhill section of Shimla. The bus raced around the curves on Cart Road and passed a railway station below the road and went by the back of Cecil Hotel, which was above the road. The thick forests along the way made it feel like evening was approaching.

When I reached Summerhill, I got off at an intersection of the highway and a narrow road that led up to HPU. I walked up the road for a short distance and then headed down a footpath to the English department. As I met familiar students, we greeted each other by saying *Hi* or *Namaste*.

One morning, I arrived just in time for my Criticism of Methodology class and slipped into a chair next to my young friend, Kamlesh. Our lecturer, Dr. Jaidev, entered the classroom and greeted us in his soft-spoken voice. Students immediately stopped their talk and said. "Good morning, Sir."

They knew that his class was a serious one. Dr. Jaidev had many published articles and spoke at various colleges and conferences. His intelligence was apparent from the first day. He was a modest man, considering his accomplishments.

Class began with Dr. Jaidev saying, "Today's discussion is about imagery in the novels we have read." He read several passages with sensory imagery and connected the imagery with the author's message. Then, Dr. Jaidev touched on color imagery.

A student in the front row asked. "Do colors have universal meanings?"

Dr. Jaidev replied, "That's a good question. Some colors have universal meanings connected with them. Also, different cultures have different meanings for colors. Each piece of literature and passage must be studied carefully to see what the author's message is for a particular color. The author doesn't always intend the universal meaning in his color imagery."

A middle-aged female student mentioned. "I always think of white as meaning purity and black as evil. How will I know if this is the author's intention in the novel I am reading?"

Dr. Jaidev explained that you have to read and reread the passage where the imagery occurs and also look at other places in the novel where the author uses the same color. He suggested that the class look at examples from the novel this student was reading and help her figure it out. These discussions made me realize that I wanted to explore color imagery for my thesis. After class, I was scheduled to meet with Dr. Jaidev to discuss my thesis. I went into his sparsely furnished office. He looked up from his work and said, "Please be seated. What thoughts do you have about your thesis?"

I told him. "I'd like to examine color imagery in a few novels. What do you think?"

He liked my idea and said that he was willing to work with me. Then he suggested some novels to read for the study and a few books on formalist studies of color imagery. Before leaving his office, he gave me *Anatomy of Criticism: Four Essays* by Northrop Frye[39] and asked me to read the book. He said, "At our next conference, we will be more specific about the process of examining color imagery."

On the way home, my mind was racing with thoughts about my thesis. Once I got home, I began by reading Frye's book and also continued reading the novel *Surfacing* by Margaret Atwood.[40] While reading her book, I wrote down my observations and questions. Then, I went back and underlined all the colors mentioned, listed them with page numbers, and wrote down the textual evidence relating to the significance of each color. Next, I organized my notes, making separate folders for each color. When this was done, I read through my notes to see if I could find patterns and meanings for the colors. It began to emerge that the different characters, scenery, and objects were represented by different colors. For instance, the heroine's friend Anna was identified with pink, an artificial color that suggested mutilation.

In contrast, the color green was a pure color, which appeared in the natural setting of *Surfacing* and was prevalent in the journey motif. For

---

[39] Princeton University Press, 1971.
[40] McClelland and Stewart, 1972.

example, the green grass suggested that the heroine should forget her difficulties of the past and let the green of nature heal her wounds. Later, the green leopard frog with black spots was a metaphor for the heroine's quest. The green of nature was a healer and helped lead the heroine from her black past to a better place. She had to be careful of green and recognize that it was only a resting place in her journey. Looking at the images for green and black, I came to the conclusion that destruction in nature was a metaphor for the heroine's damaged self.

I met with Dr. Jaidev again. He looked at my notes and liked what I told him about the use of green and black color imagery. Then he gave me some ideas about the use of "sacred red." I continued to meet with Dr. Jaidev on a weekly basis.

Then I began my study of color imagery in the novels *The Solid Mandala* by Patrick White[41] and *Herzog* by Saul Bellow.[42] I read, re-read, and took notes on the two novels. I looked at my ideas for all three books and found recurring images and patterns. Predominant recurring images were the "sacred red" in *Surfacing*, the "stripes" motif in *Herzog*, and the "orange sun" in *The Solid Mandala*. Patterns became evident in each novel. I noticed evidence of a "trail of colors" in *Surfacing*, "color conflicts" in *Herzog*, and a "multi-colored pattern" in *The Solid Mandala*.

Once I had enough notes and ideas for a rough draft, I started writing in pencil so that I could erase as needed. The beginning was tough, but after I wrote a few pages, my ideas started to flow. I followed a schedule in which I did most of my writing in the morning when I was alone in the house. After handwriting a first draft, I read it from beginning to end and made revisions.

Next, I began to type my first draft using my Remington typewriter, which had been shipped with my other belongings from the United States in 1962. With no erasing features on the typewriter, I often typed one page many times as I edited and revised. After I completed my first typewritten draft, I gave it to Dr. Jaidev. He said, "I need some time to read it. We can meet tomorrow to talk about your work."

I was surprised that he offered to meet with me the next day. Other students had complained that their advisors took weeks to get back to them.

The next day we met, and he made many suggestions. I took notes

---

[41] Viking, 1966.

[42] Viking, 1964.

My Own Return to College

as he talked. Of course, his ideas meant rereading certain passages in the three novels and some rewriting. After doing this, I brought the newly typed thesis back with the revisions I had made based on his suggestions. We went through this process several times. Finally he said, "Your thesis is ready for typing by a university typist, and then it can be submitted to an outside examiner."

I contacted the young typist and gave him my thesis. Once it was ready, Dr. Jaidev sent it to an examiner at Calcutta University. Now the waiting game started. Finally, Dr. Jaidev called me and said that the examiner was coming to Shimla, and the date for defending my thesis was scheduled for the first week of October, 1987. I started having doubts. *Would the examiner like my thesis? Would it be accepted for my MPhil degree?*

The long-awaited day arrived. It was a crisp, autumn day. Holding my thesis, I walked into the room used for student-faculty conferences and felt a sense of trepidation. A casually dressed man stood up and introduced himself. He smiled and said. "You must be Elma." Then he remarked. "Your cool Shimla weather is a welcome relief from the Calcutta heat I left behind."

His pleasant manner made me feel a little less nervous. Then he began his queries. "I have read your thesis. You have included some thought-provoking ideas. How did you choose this topic?"

For two hours we discussed my choice of the topic, the process I followed, and my conclusions. I was amazed at his detailed questions and comments. Most comments were positive, although he did say, "I would have liked more about color imagery used as metaphors."

Finally he said. "I've made a few suggestions, but I am impressed by the process you followed. It led to a clear interpretation of the color imagery in the three novels."

I had never expected such praise for my work. Then he added. "If you had submitted this as a doctoral thesis, I would have accepted it."

At first I was silent. I was shocked that he thought it was good enough for a PhD thesis requirement. Then I collected my thoughts and said. "I really appreciate your in-depth reading of my thesis, thoughtful observations, suggestions, and positive feedback. Thank you for accepting my thesis for the MPhil degree."

27

Ama-ji

On September 12, 2002 we received the heartbreaking news that Ama-ji had passed away. Now, whenever I visit our ancestral home in Mandi, it feels empty without her smiling face and caring nature.

Ama-ji was a lovely woman, both inside and out. When we first met, I immediately noticed many details: her brown eyes, black hair pulled back in a bun, short stature, the Om tattoo on her hand, and the diamond stud on the side of her nose. She almost always wore a loose-fitting *salwar kameez*. Even at night, she wore one—it was just older and less fashionable than her day attire. She was thin except for a little bit of a stomach, which was not surprising since she was the mother of three daughters and a son, each spaced about three years apart. Most of her day was spent cooking, cleaning, reading religious books, and entertaining visitors from afternoon into evening. If

Ama-ji spinning

Ama-ji

she was lucky, she squeezed in a short nap between her late lunch and the arrival of relatives and friends.

Ama-ji was married at age seven to Babu-ji, who was fourteen. However, they didn't live together as husband and wife until she was almost sixteen. When Ama-ji was first married, she visited her in-laws' house during the day and was homeschooled in reading and basic math. After a few years, she moved to her in-laws' house. For much of that period, Babu-ji was in college and then law school in Lahore, which was in India at that time. As a preteen, she learned simple cooking recipes. Throughout her life, she loved cooking. She quickly picked up everything her mother-in-law and the family cook showed her in the kitchen.

Selfless, generous, hardworking, and friendly were a few of Ama-ji's outstanding characteristics. At meal times, she was the last one to eat. She kept offering seconds and thirds even though we said. *"Bahut, Bahut!"* (Enough, enough!) When she was sure all had eaten well, she had her meal. If everyone had left the dining room, she ate in the kitchen with the young servant, who helped with cooking and cleaning.

Ama-ji read spiritual books like the *Bhagavad Gita* and *Ramayan* and said her prayers in a tiny prayer room. It had brass figures of gods and goddesses, candles in clay containers, holy books, and a small brass bell. Her daily routine was to bathe, read, pray, and cook. If her routine extended beyond noon, she skipped breakfast.

One Mandi custom that Ama-ji always observed was having her daughters and their families visit every day. Not only did they visit, but all were served a meal. They had their own homes but never missed spending a part of their day with their parents. Of course, this meant a lot of work for Ama-ji, because she did most of the cooking herself. Her young servant helped with the prep work, like removing stones from the lentils and kneading flour for *rotis*, bread. The rest of the cooking was Ama-ji's job. Her passion for cooking showed in the tastiness of her food, and she was certainly one of the best cooks in Mandi.

It was not unusual to find Ama-ji, dressed in a salwar kameez and white rubber bath slippers, sitting cross-legged on a tiny, six-inch high, wooden stool in front of a slow-burning wood fire in the Mandi, family kitchen. Whenever she was making more than fifty *kachoris*, leavened bread stuffed with ground lentils, she preferred the wood fire. It was faster, and she liked sitting on the stool for the lengthy cooking session.

Each kachori needed to be stuffed and shaped in advance so the leavened dough would rise before cooking. Then the kachoris were nestled between a blanket and a shawl in a flat, wide wicker basket. Ama-ji reached over to the basket, picked up one, and placed it on the griddle. She did the same with two more. As they started to get brown spots on the lower side, she turned them over. Once they were cooked on both sides, she took them off the griddle, and put them in the slow-burning embers of the fire to make them crisper.

Some of the kachoris were fried in a wok-like pan on the gas stove. Ama-ji usually asked her middle daughter to make the fried ones, which involved standing, so that she could remain on the floor.

Once the food was ready, she would call us to the dining room attached to the kitchen. The room was so small that the table and six chairs almost filled up the room. Ama-ji served the kachoris along with sautéed potatoes, Indian pickles, and yogurt. She was very particular to ask how we liked our kachoris cooked. Madhu loved his very crisp. Ama-ji placed his special kachori on his plate, poked holes in it, and added ghee, butter boiled until it became thick and greasy. I liked mine served with fresh butter rather than ghee. As soon as we finished one, Ama-ji was there with a second one. If we refused, she insisted and usually dropped one on our plates. Ama-ji was never satisfied until everyone had a full stomach.

Years later, when Madhu, Tara, Rita, and I moved back to the United States, Ama-ji visited us for four months. This occurred in the mid-1990s, and she was a widow at the time. The trip to America was her first. Madhu traveled to and from India with her.

Her favorite times during that visit occurred when her granddaughters, Tara and Rita, visited, and when she cooked for us. In between, she did the spinning work that she brought from India. She had a lot of spare time and finished spinning all of the raw wool into fine pashmina thread sooner than she had expected. Without any craft projects to keep her busy, she asked me to give her some knitting needles and wool to keep her occupied. Weekends we kept her busy sightseeing and visiting family and Indian friends.

Towards the end of her visit, she confessed. "When I am by myself in your home, it feels like a jail." She explained that in Mandi she was always surrounded by friends and family, especially after she finished her cooking and praying. There wasn't a day that her three daughters and their families didn't visit, along with many others. Here in New England, there were almost no visitors during the weekdays. I worked and was out of the house a good part of the day.

It was like solitary confinement for her when none of us were around. However, even though she expressed this sentiment, she was happy much of her visit, particularly when she was talking with us, cooking, and doing her crafts.

Ama-ji's only skeleton in the closet, so to speak, was the fact that she was an extreme pack rat. She stockpiled items like cooking utensils, food staples, bolts of cloth, cleaning supplies, and much more. One particular item I cannot forget was her favorite brand of brown bar soap, which was used for washing clothes. In India, whenever we were at a store that carried the soap, she said in Hindi. "Elma, let's buy ten kilos."[43]

I wondered what she did with so much soap. After her death, I went through her belongings and found large boxes of these bars of soap. They were in every closet of the house, all the bathrooms, and in many of her steel trunks.

I miss my mother-in-law. Her selflessness, generosity, and constant caring for others reminded me of a saint. We will carry her treasured memory in our hearts forever.

---

[43] 22 pounds

part V

Coming Home

28

Return to America

Living in India for twenty-five years, I experienced a journey from culture shock to biculturalism and synthesis. Friends and family in both countries often commented on how well I had assimilated. Nevertheless, I decided to return to the United States in 1987.

Why did I return to the United States? Both daughters came here for college, and I decided I wanted to try living in the United States again. *Birth roots don't go away.* Most of my American family lived in New England, and I felt my roots drawing me back.

Initially, Madhu, who fully supported my decision, stayed in India, hoping to complete the necessary years for a retirement pension. He had accumulated a lot of vacation time and could come visit for a couple of months each year. I also planned to make yearly visits to India.

When I first returned to the United States, I lived with my parents in Milford, New Hampshire, and looked for a job. My first jobs were obtained through a temp agency. I also did some substitute teaching while looking for something more permanent.

After a couple of months, I secured a job with the Cambodian Mutual Assistance Association (CMAA), a nonprofit organization in Lowell, Massachusetts. My work was mainly with Cambodian refugees, teaching them English and helping them find jobs, which allowed them to get off the temporary welfare plan they had because of their refugee status. My Indian life experiences were extremely helpful in this job. I didn't speak my students' languages, but I could identify with their adjustment struggles. Likewise, they identified with me and worked hard to do well in my class.

During my six years at the CMAA, I took graduate courses at night at Notre Dame College in Manchester, New Hampshire, and earned my second Master's degree. My new degree was Teaching English as a Second Language, and I became certified to teach second-language students in K–12 grades.

Shortly after becoming certified, I applied for a teaching job in the Lowell school system and was offered a job at the Rogers Middle School. I worked with the children of Cambodian, Laotian, and Vietnamese refugees. English was their second language, and my Indian experiences helped with positive student-teacher relationships. Working in a school, I had the summers off, and I was able to go to India for two months every year.

As soon as Madhu retired from his forestry job, he moved to the United States to be with me and the girls. I continued to work. Our circle of friends included many Indians. They were surprised by my experiences as a forestry department wife in Himachal Pradesh, my skills at Indian cooking, and how well I spoke Hindi. Yes, I had returned to the United States, but I had also retained the most precious parts of my Indian identity.

29

United States to Kulu

In October of 2011, Madhu and I made one of our yearly trips to India. Weather-wise, October was one of the best months to be in India. Previously, we had needed to schedule visits for July or August, during the monsoon season, because that's when I had time off from my teaching job in Lowell. Now that I was retired, we had flexibility for our travel dates.

We arrived at the Delhi International Airport by a British Airways flight from London at 11:35 p.m. The new, modern international airport was nothing like the Delhi airport we experienced on our first trip to India, and we immediately appreciated the air conditioning. The shops, which were multiple, were closed at this late hour, but I could see that they contained the latest technology gadgets for sale, and wireless connections were available for a fee. It was completely in line with other upscale international airports. What a difference!

It was almost 12:30 a.m. by the time we cleared security and got our luggage. Our flight to Kulu/Bhuntar Airport on Kingfisher Airlines was not set to depart until the next morning at 10:10, so we had booked a room in a nearby hotel. We went outside the terminal to find the taxi that the hotel had promised to send for us. We looked at the signs held by the receiving crowd, but there were none with our name or the hotel's name, La Sapphire. We walked up and down the street, where cars and taxis were waiting to pick up arriving passengers. No luck.

After ten minutes of searching, we booked a taxi to take us to the hotel. The driver didn't know the hotel but assured us that he could find it with the address we gave him of Mahipalpur Extension off to one side of NH 8 highway. He found the street, which was lined with hotels, but he couldn't find the hotel. After a few inquiries, we learned that it was on a small narrow side street off the main street, where we had been searching.

When we checked in, the front desk clerk said that we must have missed the hotel taxi, which he then cancelled. Our room was fifty dollars for the night, a reasonable rate. Although it was advertised as a budget hotel, our spacious second-floor room had a TV, refrigerator, coffee maker, and a large king-sized bed with clean linens. It also had an air conditioner and a fan. Both were needed. The attached bathroom was adequate, with toilet paper and a hot and cold water shower. We got into bed. It felt great to stretch out flat after nine hours of sitting on narrow airplane seats.

At six in the morning, a phone call woke us up. It was daughter Rita, calling from the U.S. to make sure we arrived safely. I had a simple breakfast of toast, cereal, and eggs in our room. Madhu was recovering from mouth cancer and couldn't eat regular food. He relied primarily on liquid nutritional supplements, such as Ensure or Boost, and pureed food. However, he was able to eat the scrambled eggs along with a jar of baby food and the Boost I had brought with us from the U.S.

At 7:50 a.m., we checked out of the hotel and hired a taxi for the ten-minute ride to the airport, where we checked our two bags. They were just under the allowance of forty-four pounds per bag. During our wait, Madhu drank his Boost before going through security. Due to airline regulations, carrying liquid Boost in his handbag was a problem, but he was allowed to take his baby food when we showed it to a security official and explained the situation.

After clearing security, we found out that our flight was delayed until 11:25 a.m. This meant there was time to check out the shopping area. We were amazed at the availability of the latest technology products: Smartphones, iPads, and much more. In the food court, there were places that served a variety of Indian and Western food. I had a cup of espresso coffee. Then I paid to hook up to the internet and checked my email.

The restrooms throughout the airport were clean and had toilet paper. As we sat near the departure gate, we chatted with another passenger, who told us that it was possible to pay ten dollars an hour at the airport for a chair bed and the use of a toilet and shower. We decided that we might try this arrangement on our next visit, especially if our layover time was shorter.

Finally, our flight left at 11:30. It was a twenty-four passenger airplane, and all the seats were occupied. For most of the one-hour flight, we could see the ground below us. The view was spectacular, particularly as we flew above the motor road from Mandi to Kulu. We saw the winding river below, green trees on the mountain side, and familiar tea stalls along the road.

The most amazing sight appeared shortly before we landed at Bhuntar. The plane made a half-turn and flew into a valley between two mountain ridges. We looked down from our window and recognized several friends' homes. There were pedestrians, cars, busses, and motorcycles travelling on the narrow, curvy road. Apple orchards were visible on the mountain side above the road.

Immediately after passing Bajaura, we landed safely and walked into the tiny airport to collect our luggage. Only passengers were allowed inside the airport. We looked outside and saw Madhu's faithful friend Rajinder waiting for us. On leaving the airport, we warmly greeted each other, walked about forty feet to Rajinder's medium-sized car, and set off on a five-minute ride to his Bajaura home for a short stopover.

After Indian tea and fifteen minutes of nonstop talk with Rajinder and his wife, Santosh, Rajinder called his driver and sent us to our final destination, Mandi. The ride from Bajaura to Mandi took ninety minutes. Traveling on familiar roads and passing homes we had seen from the plane window, time went by quickly.

View of Mandi town

30

Stay at Mandi

After the ninety-minute ride from Bajaura, our driver pulled up to a narrow gully with shops on both sides. We were almost at our ancestral home in Mandi, Himachal Pradesh. Madhu owned half of the home, which he had inherited after the death of his parents. This was as far as the car could go. Waiting in front of a small shop was Cha-

Narrow street along our Mandi home

Stay at Mandi

man, a young man who had worked many years for us and was now employed by the forest department. He was with Chintha and her two teenage sons, who lived in our home and took care of the house while we were away. All touched our feet to show their respect.

They quickly picked up our luggage and took it to our home while we went to Madhu's sister's home, which was nearby. We climbed a narrow steep staircase to Anjana's portion of her late husband's house, which was on the fourth floor. Family members—niece Minu, nephew Pnu, his wife Ritu, sister's son Raman, his daughter Radha, his son Yukteshwar, sister Hansa, brother-in-law Suresh, and sister Anjana—warmly welcomed us. Madhu's sister Hansa and her family lived in a separate house a half mile away. We enjoyed a late lunch of rice, lentils, *jhord* (buttermilk curry), and *matar panir* (peas and Indian cheese).

Anjana in her Mandi kitchen

Food on the table at Anjana's house

After lunch we asked Anjana for the keys to our third and fourth floor flat, said goodbye, left Anjana's home, and walked to our home. The ancestral home had four floors with separate living quarters. Each floor of our portion had bedrooms, a bathroom, a living room, and a kitchen. We owned half of the house, including our flat on the third and fourth floors, and the other half was owned by Madhu's cousins. His cousins had also added third and fourth floor flats on their portion of the house. Chintha and her family lived in a portion of the lower floor and were the caretakers. While we were away for eleven months each year, they kept an eye on everything. During our visits they helped with cleaning, washing clothes, and general domestic work. They had a few rooms on the first floor.

Painting the 2nd floor balcony of Mandi ancestral home

We entered the house through an elaborately carved wooden door that was kept open during the day and locked at night. We walked a short distance on the maroon cement floors and climbed a flight of ancient stairs, which were almost like a wooden ladder. Then we climbed the second set of stairs, which was wider, much newer, and made of cement. We reached our flat and saw our luggage piled up by the locked door.

Chintha's sons helped carry our bags into the dining-living room. Chintha had cleaned the rooms before our arrival, and Chaman had made up our bed with clean sheets and a turquoise quilt. The refrigerator was stocked with milk, eggs, boiled water, bread, and other necessities for our morning coffee, breakfast, and afternoon tea.[44]

After unpacking, I went into our tiny kitchen and tried to light the gas stove. It wouldn't start, and after several tries I realized that there was a leak in the pipe that connected the gas cylinder to the double-burner gas stove. The electric heater was working, so I could make tea, coffee, and boil water for drinking. After a short rest, we had tea and then got ready to go for dinner.

The walk to Hansa's house was up and down the footpaths of the town, and occasionally a speeding motorcyclist startled us. I wondered why they were allowed on the footpaths. We crossed a narrow bridge over the Beas River and saw ancient temples above and below the bridge. Suresh, Hansa's husband, and his grandson Yukteshwar greeted us as we climbed up the steep stairs to their house. Once inside, we were greeted by our friend Ashwani Kapur. He was about to retire from his local position of Divisional Commissioner with the Indian Administrative Service, so we knew that this was the last time we'd meet him in Mandi.

---

[44] We ate lunches at Anjana's house and had dinners at the home of Hansa, Madhu's youngest sister.

Stay at Mandi

Madhu's nephew Pnu, his wife, Ritu, their son Rishi, Madhu's niece Minu, and Minu's husband Gangesh were also there in the large living room. Anjana did not come for dinner because her husband, Ishwar-ji, had passed away in January, and she followed the Mandi custom, in which widows did not go out of their homes for one year.

We had a tasty, home-cooked meal and lots of good talk. We didn't leave the house until after ten p.m. We walked back to our house, a distance of a half mile along narrow footpaths, which were partially lit by lights coming from the houses along the way. At times a flashlight was helpful.

The next morning I planned to get a haircut. I had skipped my last American haircut so I could have it cut in Mandi. There were many shops in the lower floors of the houses along the road that led to the center of town, and I could see the haircutting salon from our open balcony. By eight a.m., I figured the salon was open, so I went down two flights of stairs to the road leading to the shop. I had guessed correctly, and my favorite hairdresser had just finished with a customer. He led me to the vacated chair and asked in Hindi, "How do you want your hair cut?"

I said in Hindi. "Cut it a half-inch shorter, and in layers. Please make sure my ears are covered."

After cutting my hair, he started massaging my head, which I loved. He finished by blow-drying my hair. My haircut looked very professional.

I asked him. "How much do I owe you?"

He replied. "Seventy rupees."[45]

I gave him the seventy rupees with a twenty rupee tip,[46] nearly thirty percent. Many Indians are not so generous with their tips, yet the total was still a little less than two dollars. My hairdresser thanked me for the tip, although he didn't show much expression. Maybe he was used to getting this kind of tip from me. After my haircut, I went back to the house and had breakfast.

Madhu and I finished unpacking, organized our closets, and made lists of tasks that needed to be done. The first job was to get Chaman to fix the gas pipe. He arrived at our flat at nine, before going to the forestry office where he worked as a *peon*, an office attendant. He looked at the pipe and said that it needed to be replaced. He bought a new pipe in a shop near our house, hooked it up, and the gas stove worked fine.

---

[45] One dollar and thirty-five cents

[46] Thirty-five cents

My next projects were to go through the many rooms in our section of the house, check for moths in trunks and closets, give away things we didn't use, and do the cleaning jobs that were missed by Chintha. I started with our third-floor rooms. After working an hour, I'd had enough. I decided to do an hour each day. It was a big job.

Now I was ready to venture into town to look for an internet connection for my Acer laptop, which I had brought from the United States. On our way into town, Madhu and I met Rajinder and his son Sanju, and they accompanied us to the shop. We talked with the shopkeeper and showed him my laptop. He started setting it up with a Tata proton connection. We bought the flash drive for 1,700 rupees[47] and paid a connection fee of 225 rupees.[48] I tried the connection in the shop and was able to get online. The young shopkeeper assured us it would work throughout India.

We immediately went home and looked for a convenient place to plug the computer in using the 210-to-110 transformer. After trying several places, I decided to use the dining room table. I turned the connection on, went online, and checked email. Having a wireless internet connection at home was a first. Previously I had used internet cafes, which were slow and didn't always work.

After some bank work the next day, we started visiting our close relatives. We walked to the home of Madhu's two uncles. First we visited his elder uncle and aunt who lived in the upper portion of the house. In accordance with the Mandi custom, we brought them fruit, biscuits, bread, and butter.

Then we went downstairs to visit with Madhu's younger uncle and aunt and gave them the same food items as we had given upstairs. We particularly enjoyed speaking with their son Sanjeev, nicknamed Jippu, who had been a doctor in the local government hospital and now worked for a private hospital. He continued to do orthopedic surgery in the private hospital and also drew a government pension. Our conversation with Sanjeev was upbeat, but things changed when his dad came into the room. Uncle was depressed about his physical condition and was crying about life in general. His wife had her own health problems but was quite positive about life. She kept offering us food and tea, but we insisted that we didn't want anything to eat or drink.

---

[47] Thirty-one dollars

[48] Four dollars

On October ninth we attended a G-11 dinner party with a group of Madhu's eleven friends and their spouses. The get-together was at the Riverside Hotel Restaurant located above the Sakethi River. The luncheon was hosted by P.C. Sharma and his wife. Mrs. P.C. called us the day before and asked what food Madhu could eat. She said she'd bring two vegetables cooked at her home with no chilies and according to Madhu's dietary needs, due to his surgeries for mouth cancer. We played *tambola*, a game similar to bingo. I called the numbers for one of the games. After our games, we did a lot of catching up with our friends and had a sumptuous lunch.

The following day, we continued our visits to relatives and friends. Our first visit was with Dr. Jyoti, who was a retired doctor and a widower. He lived with his son and two daughters-in-law. We went to pay our condolences for the recent death of his son Prakash. Dr. Jyoti was in amazing physical and mental condition for being ninety-four. He was a positive person and pleased to see us. His daughters-in-law kept offering snacks and tea, even when we insisted that we didn't want anything to eat or drink.

Elma taking pictures with her iPad

From Dr. Jyoti's home, we went to Rajinder's house, which was further down the road. He had physical problems and was on dialysis twice a week in a private Mandi hospital which cost about 30,000 rupees[49] a month. He hoped that part of it would be reimbursed through his wife's health benefits, since she was a retired government lady doctor. Rajinder had been a life insurance salesman and owned an apple orchard in Bajaura, which his son managed.

During this visit, we particularly noticed that as our friends and relatives grew older, they faced more and more health problems. However, they were fortunate to have family who lived with them and gave them a great deal of support. It was another real strength of the traditional Indian way of life.

Madhu outside of girl's high school, Mandi

---

[49] $555.00

Jogindernagar Visit

After lunch on October 17, Madhu and I left for Jogindernagar to visit our nephew Pnu and his wife Ritu. We traveled from Mandi to Jogindernagar in Pnu's government station-wagon jeep. He had been at Shimla and Mandi for work and was returning to his headquarters at Jogindernagar.

The trip took two hours on a narrow, winding mountain road. The weather was quite warm so we used the air conditioning, which meant we kept the windows closed and didn't have to deal with dust from the road. There was a lot of traffic as we got close to Jogindernagar, and when we reached town our jeep came to a standstill along with many large trucks, school buses, cars, jeeps, and motorcycles, due to some cows that were blocking traffic.

We finally made it through town and started down the mountain road to Pnu and Ritu's home in the Himachal Electricity Board Colony. When we reached the house at three p.m., Pnu went straight to his office, which was across the street.

Their home was a large, two-story, government house with a well-kept, fenced yard. It had a gate with a large sign: *Harish Malhotra, Deputy Chief Engineer*. Next to the house was a garage, where they kept their private car and government vehicle.

Since it was still mid-afternoon, Madhu and I decided to take a walk. We asked Ritu where we should go, and she suggested that we walk down the hill towards a village about a half-mile away. I changed into my walking shoes and headed out with Madhu. A bus and two jeeps passed us on our way down the narrow road. We reached a bridge at a section of the road that leveled off and then returned home. The fall weather was refreshing and warm. Neither of us wore sweaters or jackets. The walk felt good after the two hour jeep ride.

We got back to the house and had tea with Pnu and Ritu. Then we discussed food for our evening meal, especially what Madhu could eat. Ritu asked. "I plan to make Indian cheese, bread stuffed with potatoes, yellow lentils, and a soft vegetable. I have ice cream that I bought in town. Is everything okay?"

I replied. "It sounds good to me."

Next, we made our bed up for the night in

Elma on the Jogindarnagar walk to Majharnoo

the ground floor, guest bedroom. The attractive sheets Ritu gave us for the bed were machine-embroidered in pastel colors. The pillowcases had matching embroidery. When we first came to India all the sheets were plain white sheets. I still have a set of the white sheets that Tara brought with her when she came to the U.S. for college.

Madhu and I returned to the living room, and the men had beer and scotch. All of us had light snacks followed by homemade soup. I was happy with just the snacks and soup, but we were then served a full-course meal.

Next morning, we were up early after a comfortable sleep in the king-sized bed. Fresh air streamed into the room from the open windows. Our room had a large attached bathroom with a toilet, sink, and boiler to heat water for our Indian bucket showers. I turned the boiler on and went into the kitchen to make coffee rather than bed tea, which was served in the bedroom by servants or the woman of the house. While drinking my coffee, I made Madhu's oatmeal for breakfast.

After I had made the oatmeal, Ritu came into the kitchen. She remarked. "You managed well with the coffee and oatmeal."

I complimented her. "It's easy working in your organized, well-stocked kitchen. It's so much better than the kitchens I had when I first came to India."

"Thanks Auntie."

While drinking my second cup of coffee, I tried to connect to the internet on my laptop. Yesterday, I had been unable to get on. Today, the Tata Proton wireless connection still didn't work. I kept getting error 678. Ritu told me that they often experienced connectivity problems with their son Rishi's laptop and sometimes with their cell phones.

Pnu said. "I think there is a problem with your connection. It must not be set up for roaming wireless. I'll call Rishi and see what he suggests."

When Pnu called Rishi, he made some suggestions. They didn't resolve the connectivity problem at the time, but later I was able to get online.

After our morning showers, Ritu served us a home-cooked, South Indian breakfast of *upama* (cream of wheat with grated vegetables in it). She also cut up papaya for me and ground it for Madhu. The Indian papaya was much tastier than any papaya I've had in the United States.

Pnu told us. "I will send my jeep in the afternoon, and Ritu will take you for an outing to see the local attractions. I can't go with you because I have too much work at the office."

I said. "That's fine. It will give us time to take our morning walk."

At about 10:00, Madhu and I went for our walk in the same direction as yesterday. We headed towards the village of Majharnoo. After crossing the bridge, we passed a small rain shelter, which was also a bus stop. Just beyond the shelter, there was a road off to the left. We took it and walked towards a large house about a one-quarter of a mile up the road. On the way, we passed two laborers building a small brick house right next to the road.

Some of the houses had cars parked beside them. We continued walking until we reached the driveway of a large, two-story building, which was much grander than the other houses on the road. We guessed it must be the home of Gulab Singh, a political minister.

We returned to the bus stand, and I told Madhu. "I want to walk down the main road and take pictures of the animals I see in the distance." Madhu waited for me at the bus stop. He got tired of all my picture taking and was happy to take a rest. I took pictures of a mother cow and her baby for our grandchildren who loved animals.

Jogindernagar Visit

Then I saw a village school below the road. Children were outside for a recess break between classes. I took pictures of the kids and the school sign. A young man came out and in a friendly tone asked. "What's your good name?"

I told him who I was, and that I was visiting family in Jogindernagar.

He introduced himself. "I'm Mr. Sharma, the headmaster of the school."

He invited me into his office and told me that the school was for sixth to tenth standard (grade) boys and girls. It was a Hindi-medium school, but they were working on teaching science subjects in English. One of the teachers came into the office, and Mr. Sharma introduced him as a science teacher.

They offered me tea, but I politely refused. However, when Mr. Sharma asked me if I'd like to visit the classrooms, I replied. "I'd love to."

The headmaster began the tour of the school by showing me the new public address system, which he was very proud of. We went into a break room, and he introduced me to the male and female teachers. All were cordial and friendly. A bell rang and classes resumed. First, we visited a math classroom. Students were a little shy, but as I spoke to them in Hindi they started to talk with me. They all wore school uniforms. The girls wore a blue *kameez* (long shirt) over a white *salwar* (pajama like pant), and the boys had on white pants or pajamas and a blue shirt. Then we went into a science lab. It was pretty basic, with just a few tables with some beakers, scales, and measuring sticks on them.

Next we went into the tenth standard English classroom. I asked a lot of questions and requested a young girl to show me her textbook. One of the stories they were reading was *The Diary of Anne Frank*. I told the class. "My students in America read and act out this play."

After visiting other classrooms and being warmly received, I said. "I really enjoyed my visit, but I need to leave, because my husband is waiting for me at the bus stop and doesn't know where I am."

The headmaster insisted. "You must return to my office and sign the guest book."

I agreed. After signing, he once again offered me tea.

Again I refused. "I really need to leave."

He quickly took out a plate of cashew nuts from a large, wooden cabinet and offered them to me. I thanked him for the tour of the school and rushed back to the bus stop, where Madhu was waiting. He had guessed that I was visiting the school, because a village woman had told him that there was a school down the road, and she saw a foreign lady taking pictures there.

We started our walk back to the house. It was a steady climb, but the weather was so pleasant we didn't feel tired. On our way, we heard a motorcycle approaching from behind. The cycle stopped, and it was the headmaster of the school.

I introduced Madhu to Mr. Sharma, and we talked for a while. He confirmed that Minister Gulab Singh lived in the large house, we had guessed was the minister's. Mr. Sharma couldn't say enough about the many helpful things Gulab Singh had done for his school. Then he rode off, and in about five minutes we were back at the house.

After lunch Ritu, Madhu, and I went for a ride in Pnu's government jeep to see some of the Jogindernagar sights. The government driver drove up a hill to Chaprot, where electricity was generated by the Punjab Electricity board. The power station was originally constructed by British officers and Indian workers during the British Raj. The narrow road was paved when we started out, but as we got closer to the power station, there were stretches that needed repaving, and there were lots of ruts. In places the road was so narrow that only one vehicle could travel on it at a time. If we met another vehicle, we had to slow down and find a place where the road was wide enough to cross.

We reached the power station, and a security guard stopped us at the gate. At first, he said that we couldn't enter, but when we told him who we were he allowed us to go into the power station and dam area. We got out of our jeep and walked around. I took pictures of the dam, water pipes, mountain views, and the valley below us. The hillside was covered with deodar and conifer trees.

We left the Punjab Electricity project and rode down the mountain towards the town of Jogindernagar and then on to Machal village. The village was about a half mile below Pnu's office complex. Ritu told us. "There is a stream that runs below Machal that has trout fish. Many people come to see the jumping fish. They consider it a holy place and come to pray along the stream."

Shortly before we reached the bridge leading to Machal, we saw clouds of smoke in the sky. As we got closer to the village, there were blazing red flames shooting out from one of the houses. We started to cross the bridge and were shocked to see the house engulfed in flames. There were many bystanders standing around watching the burning house. Only two people were carrying buckets from a water tank nearby and throwing water on the flames. I couldn't believe that everybody

Jogindernagar Visit

else was just watching. I wondered why they didn't make a line from the nearby stream, pass buckets of water up to the burning house, and then throw them on the flames.

As we got closer to the fire, we saw that all the wooden windows and doors of the house were badly burnt, but the mud walls were mostly intact. The roof was partially burnt. A bystander told us in Hindi. "The fire started from an exploded gas cylinder in the kitchen of the house. Fire trucks have been called, and we are waiting for the firemen to put the fire out."

Fire in village Machal below Jogindernagar

Realizing there wasn't much we could do, we looked down at the stream to see if there were any jumping fish. We didn't see any. Ritu said. "It's probably too late in the day to see them. I think they only jump in the bright sunlight."

We started back to the house and on the way were relieved to meet a fire truck headed towards the fire.

That evening during cocktail hour, we told Pnu about our trip. I said. "I was shocked that the Machal villagers did so little to help put the fire out."

He defended the villagers. "They must have figured that they couldn't do anything to help and knew the fire truck was coming."

Then we started talking about our plans for the following day's trip to Dharamsala where Madhu had been posted two times, once as Divisional Forest Officer and the second time when he was promoted to the position of Conservator of Forests.

32

Day Trip to Dharamsala Area

After helping Ritu make cucumber, cheese, and tomato sandwiches for our day trip to Dharamsala and McLeod Gunj, I packed the sandwiches along with boiled water, Madhu's emergency food of Boost and baby food, and our camera. Madhu and I left the house at nine in a taxi arranged by Pnu. We planned to meet our friend Gurdeep Singh, a forest contractor from Pathankot, at the Daulhadhar Tourist Lodge in the main bazaar of Dharamsala at noon.

After leaving Jogindernagar, we passed Chauntra, Bajnath, and Parola. About halfway to Dharamsala, there was a roadblock, and vehicles were at a standstill. We got out of our taxi, walked a short distance, and saw that the public works department laborers were tarring the road. We watched them, took pictures, and after ten minutes the traffic started moving again.

Shortly before reaching Dharamsala, we stopped at Siddhbardhi to visit Sacred Heart School, where Rita and Tara had been students in fourth and sixth standards in 1978. Initially, they had been day students, but when Madhu was transferred back to Chamba, they had finished the year as boarders. They were only in boarding school for a couple of months and adjusted well. Some of the students in the school had been boarders from the time they were in first standard since their parents lived in places where there were no English medium schools.

Our taxi parked outside the school gates, and we walked into the school grounds, where an outdoor assembly was in progress. Students and teachers stood in an open athletic field as the principal addressed them. A security guard approached us and told us that we had to get permission to visit the school.

We watched the assembly and then crossed the open ground to the office, where we talked to the secretary. She told us the principal was Sister Theresa Thomas, a nun from Kerala, and we had to wait to meet her before we could tour the school. We went back outside and watched the assembly. It ended soon, and the uniformed students returned to their classrooms in an orderly manner. The principal immediately went to her office.

We went back to the receptionist's desk, and she led us into the principal's spacious office. We sat in front of her large desk and introduced ourselves as parents of former Sacred Heart students. She told us we could walk around the outside of the school, but we could not go in the buildings or take pictures of students. I was disappointed that we couldn't go into the classrooms. After talking a little more with her, I realized that she was busy, and we needed to visit the school on our own. We walked around the outside of the buildings. Some were new, and some were the same as when Tara and Rita had studied there. Off to one side, we saw students doing exercises in a large athletic field. Then we left the school.

I was disappointed by the school visit and the principal's indifference, especially since a few days earlier I had been so warmly welcomed at the Jogindernagar government school. There, I didn't know anyone but had been escorted by the headmaster throughout the school and into the classrooms. Here, at the private convent school where Tara and Rita had been students, I was on my own and wasn't invited into classrooms to meet students and to talk with teachers.

We quickly went back to our taxi and started out for Dharamsala to meet Gurdeep. After five minutes on the road, we received a call on our cell phone from Gurdeep, who was at the tourist lodge fifteen minutes early. Shortly before reaching Dharamsala, we saw the impressive, new cricket stadium about a mile from the main road. As we came to the outskirts of the town, we drove by many familiar landmarks. We passed the civil hospital, the forest colony where we used to live, *Kanchi Mordh* (a sharp turn shaped like a pair of open scissors), and the old bus stand. Finally, we drove into the parking lot of the tourist lodge, parked our taxi, asked the driver to wait for us, and went inside.

Gurdeep Singh was waiting for us in the lobby. We talked for a while and then left for McLeod Ganj, with Gurdeep joining us in our taxi.

Most of the trip was on a steep road, which leveled off just before McLeod Ganj. We saw a new, covered parking garage with several levels. Our taxi driver parked the taxi, and we gave him money for his lunch.

We walked toward the bazaar and passed many foreigners. Most were wearing Indian or Tibetan clothes. Our plan was to visit the Tibetan carpet factory first. I used to purchase rugs from this factory for my carpet export business.[50] However, when we arrived at the factory, it was closed. We soon found out that there was a prayer session at the nearby residence of the Dali Lama in memory of a Tibetan nun, who had recently killed herself in Tibet to show her support for the movement to free Tibet from China. Many Tibetans left Tibet when the Chinese took over and settled in the mountainous areas of India where the climate was similar to their homeland. As we walked through the bazaar, we realized that all the Tibetan shops were closed. The only shops open were those not owned by Tibetans.

Since we were feeling hungry, we decided to have lunch at a large Chinese and Tibetan restaurant. We climbed up the stairs to the second-floor restaurant and were seated. I noticed that most of the customers were foreigners. A waiter came to take our order, and we asked if there was anything on the menu that didn't have chilies. He suggested tomato soup, so we ordered the soup for Madhu.

We told the waiter that Madhu had his own food with him because of medical reasons and asked if he could eat his jar of baby food and drink his Boost. The waiter was fine with this. Gurdeep and I shared Chinese noodles, Tibetan noodles, and *momos*, dumplings stuffed with meat. After lunch we walked through the bazaar and saw a couple of Tibetan ladies sitting on the side of the road preparing momos over an open fire and selling them.

Then we visited the Tibetan temple. It too was closed in honor of the Tibetan nun, so we walked around the outside of the temple, spun the turnstile cylinders along the sides of the temple, and took pictures.

Next, I wanted to buy some jewelry. The first shop we visited was a small, narrow store near the Tibetan rug factory. There were two shopkeepers in the store, and the jewelry was displayed on three walls and a counter. I picked out a garnet necklace, a blue bead necklace, and an amber bead one. The shopkeeper named a price, and I made a much

---

[50] While Madhu was posted at Chamba as Divisional Forest Office I started a small Tibetan carpet export business. I bought hand loomed carpets from Dalhousie and Dharamsala which I exported to the U.S. and sold some to friends and my sister Barbara.

Day Trip to Dharamsala Area

lower offer. Eventually he came close to my price and said. "This is my lowest offer. Do you want the three pieces?"

At this point Gurdeep piped in. "Just accept her price."

Reluctantly the shopkeeper agreed.

When I looked carefully at the garnet necklace, I noticed it was strung on a flimsy thread. I mentioned this to the shopkeeper.

He said. "I can restring the beads while you wait."

I agreed and watched the two shopkeepers re-thread the beads. Each one worked from opposite ends of a strong, nylon thread as they put on one bead at a time. It took longer than we expected, so we talked with the owner of the shop and learned that he was a Muslim from Kashmir.

Necklace display in a shop in McLeod Ganj

When the beads were ready, we paid for them and went to a second shop. Again we bargained in the same manner, with Gurdeep jumping in when the shopkeeper wouldn't lower the price any more. I bought a turquoise necklace with large, irregular, turquoise stones and a blue bead necklace.

On our way back to the parking garage, Madhu wanted to stop at a liquor store to see if they had red wine. After my jewelry shopping, I couldn't refuse his request. He found two bottles of red wine he liked and bought them. Of course, they were more expensive than his favorite low-priced, Trader Joe's wine, which he often bought in the United States. We got back to the parking garage, and our driver was waiting for us in the car.

We drove down the mountain to Dharamsala and stopped to take a pic-

Church on the road from McLeod Ganj to Dharamsala

ture of an old stone Christian church in the woods along the road. At Dharamsala we pulled into the tourist lodge parking lot, and Gurdeep told us to wait a minute. He went to his taxi and came back with a box of Indian sweets from a well-known Pathankot sweet shop. We said our goodbyes and headed off in opposite directions.

As we drove down from the bazaar and made a sharp left turn at Kanchi Mord, I asked to stop at the forest colony where we used to live when Madhu was Divisional Forest Officer (D.F.O.) Dharamsala. I directed the driver to our previous residence, got out of the jeep, and stood at the closed gate.

Our previous residence in Dharamsala

As I was looking at the familiar house, a man appeared from the back of the house and came to the gate. He seemed to be the caretaker. I introduced myself, and told him that I used to live in this house. Then I asked. "D.F.O. *sahib kaha hai?*" ("Where is the respected D.F.O.?")

He said that the D.F.O. was away on vacation. I asked in Hindi. "Is it okay for me to walk around the compound and take a few pictures?"

He was fine with that. I took pictures, thanked him, and got back in the jeep. We left Dharamsala and didn't make any more stops on the way back. Around 6:30 it got dark, and forty-five minutes later we reached Jogindernagar. Ritu and Pnu were waiting for us, and for the next several hours we couldn't stop talking to them about our nostalgic trip.

The next day, Madhu and I took our morning walk to Majharnoo village. After returning I continued to read *Cave in the Snow* by Vicki Mackenzie,[51] a nonfiction book written by an English woman who spent twelve years in a cave near Lahaul Spiti, became a Buddhist nun, and now lived near Palampur. I stopped reading when I heard Pnu's cough and went into the dining room. Ritu served homemade Chinese noodles for lunch, and we prepared to leave for Mandi. As we said our goodbyes, I realized just how much we'd miss Ritu's gourmet cooking, Pnu's animated convent-school English, our village walks, and the Jogindernagar area sights.

---

[51] Bloomsbury USA, 1998.

33

Raj Kumar's Mandi Visit

A whirlwind of activities kept Madhu and me busy during the rest of our 2011 visit to Mandi. There were parties to attend, club functions, shopping trips, visits with friends, dinners with relatives, and funeral services.

One morning, after returning from a shopping trip at the bazaar, I had a pleasant surprise. As I entered our ancestral home, there were many people sitting on the maroon cement verandah floor taking part in a prayer service for a recently deceased relative. I noticed a familiar out-of-town visitor sitting with friends and relatives. Raj Kumar stood up and touched my feet, followed by a young boy, who also touched my feet. I didn't recognize the boy.

The familiar face was Raj Kumar, who had started working for us at the age of twelve as a personal servant. At that time, he had completed one year of school in a small village six miles from Chamba, near where Madhu worked as Divisional Forest Officer. While serving us, Raj Kumar attended school part-time and eventually passed the fifth standard.

Preparing food for a prayer session at Mandi house

He was our private, personal attendant until he was nineteen. It took time, but eventually he became proficient at cleaning, cooking food, washing clothes, shopping for groceries, and gardening. His work ethic was excellent, and he was extremely honest. He always put our needs above his own. During the time Madhu was posted at Shimla, he was able to get Raj Kumar employed by the forest department as a *peon*, office attendant. After he was hired, he continued to work in our Shimla flat doing household chores.

Raj Kumar and his son Tushar during their Mandi visit

Every year when we visited Mandi from America, Raj Kumar learned of our trip and came to see us from Chamba, where he now worked. This time he was with a young boy, whom he introduced in Hindi. "Please meet my son, Tushar Kapoor."

I was surprised at the introduction, since the previous year, Raj Kumar and his wife had been childless. I guessed that this shy, smiling boy was adopted but waited to ask when Tushar wasn't around.

Then I said. "Please take your bags up to the top floor. Both of you will be comfortable in the sunroom with its attached bathroom."

Later in the day I suggested to Raj Kumar that he come upstairs and leave Tushar to read his book in the living room. I asked about Tushar. Raj Kumar explained. "Tushar is my brother's son. My wife and I are raising him as our son. He is ten years old."

I commented. "Tushar seems extremely attached to you, his new dad. Have you adopted him officially?"

"What do you mean?"

"You need to consult a lawyer at Chamba, and he will help you with the court adoption process."

"Why should I do this? My brother has many children and wants me to have Tushar."

"It's good to have an official adoption. As a government servant, you have many benefits for your child, but they won't be available without an official adoption. For example, if he falls sick, his medical expenses will only be reimbursed if he is your adopted son. Otherwise,

Raj Kumar's Mandi Visit

you will have to pay yourself. This could be a huge expense if Tushar became seriously ill."

Raj Kumar listened attentively but didn't say whether he planned to follow my suggestion.

That evening, we all went to Hansa and Suresh's house for dinner. Yukteshwar, Hansa's grandson, was friendly with Tushar. They played ball games while the adults talked. At the end of the evening, twelve-year-old Yukteshwar picked up the car keys and took Tushar out to the garage. Both got in the car. Yukteshwar sat in the driver's seat and backed the car out of the family garage. Tushar looked at him and said in Hindi. "Wow, you're a good driver."

Yukteshwar replied, "Thanks. Driving at twelve is illegal, so I only drive on our property."

The next day was Diwali, the festival of lights. We weren't celebrating Diwali this year because of the death of Madhu's cousin Salochana. Raj Kumar decided to take Tushar to the bazaar to see the Diwali festivities.

When they returned from the market, Tushar showed us his Diwali purchases. He excitedly told us. "I loved walking through the town and watching children setting off firecrackers. I never saw a Diwali like this one. You must go to the bazaar and see the decorations and fireworks."

Diwala trinkets for sale at Mandi

In the evening, we all left for our usual family dinner. Along the way fireworks boomed loudly, and they lit up the sky. Crowds of people dressed in their best clothes were roaming around the bazaar making purchases. Out-of-town merchants sat on the ground of the main street and spread out their Diwali trinkets on large pieces of cloth or plastic. Many shoppers kneeled on the ground to see the clay pots for incense, colorful paintings, and fireworks. Others entered the well-stocked, local stores and bought kitchen utensils, household goods, flat-screen televisions, gold, and clothes. Gold sales always skyrocketed during Diwali festivities.

When we arrived at Hansa and Suresh's home, a large group of men, women, and children were praying in the *bhajan* (prayer) hall. After a while, the women got up and walked from room to room, lighting candles and incense in small clay pots. Each clay pot had a walnut next to it.[52] Then we returned to the prayer hall, where the men were singing and praying, led by nephew Raman and his wife Suman. Many of the prayers were in Sanskrit, which I didn't understand.

When the prayers ended, we had a delicious dinner of *bhaturas* (Indian bread), *kadoo ka khatta* (pumpkin in a sweet-and-sour sauce), potato and tomato curry, *dahi bhalla* (yogurt with lentils in the shape of a doughnut), and *kheer* (rice pudding). Shortly after dinner, Yukteshwar backed the car out of the garage, and Suresh drove us home.

The next evening Raj Kumar and Tushar were to return to Chamba by the Himachal Road Transport Corporation night bus, which departed from Mandi at seven p.m. for the fourteen-hour overnight trip. Before leaving, Raj Kumar asked. "When is your next visit?"

I replied. "It will probably be a year from now."

On hearing this Raj Kumar broke into tears and couldn't stop crying. He clearly missed us as much as we missed him. Then Raj Kumar and Tushar touched our feet, picked up their luggage, and left for the bus stop.

---

[52] The hard shell of the walnut represens a person's ego, which needs to be broken to get to the true self.

34

Sharing the Draft of My Memoir with Indian Family and Friends

In March of 2012, I packed a red, loose-leaf binder in my suitcase for our yearly trip to India. I wondered if family and friends would read any of the twenty-five memoir chapters I'd completed, and if they did, what would their comments be?

For our first four days in India, Madhu and I stayed in Chandigarh with our nephew Unu, his wife, Neerja, and their son Nikhil. They lived in a small, two-bedroom, rented house. Nikhil gave up his bedroom for us and slept on a mattress on the living room floor. I felt bad for him, but he was fine with the arrangement.

The second day of our stay, I placed the binder with my memoir chapters on the living room coffee table. When nobody noticed it, I explained that I was writing a memoir about my life in India and wondered if they wanted to look at it. I mentioned that Unu was in a few chapters. All of the family said that they wanted to read it. Turn by turn, they read different chapters and made comments.

Unu loved the chapters "Uprooted," "Shimla: A Long Wait for a Job," and "Bumpy Bus Ride in the Mountains." He said that the stories brought back memories of meeting us in Delhi, our stay at Shimla with his family, and the problematic bus ride from Shimla to Rohru.

Neerja mentioned. "I laughed when I read that Unu talked with you using his convent-school English." She said that she related to my chapter "Special Delivery at Snowdon Hospital." She is not from Mandi and is not used to their customs. My story reminded her of when she had her son Nikhil in the Mandi hospital. She felt the same lack of privacy that I mentioned in my chapters.

She appreciated the chapter on "Ama-ji" and remembered her hoarding habits, especially the stockpiling of laundry soap. She asked. "Do you still find the soap in your ancestral house?"

I said. "Yes, and I give it to the washerwoman for washing our clothes."

Nikhil thought "Uprooted" and "Bumpy Bus Ride in the Mountains" were fascinating. He loved the word pictures of his dad, grandparents, and other relatives. He knew that his dad was close to Madhu but didn't realize how much time they had spent together.

From Chandigarh, Unu, Nikhil, Neerja, Madhu, and I traveled together by taxi to Mandi. It was a seven-hour ride, and one stretch of the road was extremely bumpy with huge potholes. We talked about the memoir, and how I dealt with Indian life.

After two days in Mandi, I took my binder to my sister-in-law Anjana's house, where we ate lunch every day. Once again, I explained that I'd like the family to read some of the chapters. My nephew Pnu and his son Rishi said that they wanted to read the stories. Rishi suggested I send some chapters to him through Google Chrome.

Anjana said. "I want to read the stories, if there are any in Hindi. I can't understand English."

I told her. "You know that I can't write in Hindi."

Rishi read several of the stories that covered my first year in India. His comments were positive, and he said. "I didn't know many of the things you described."

Next, I took my memoir to my sister-in-law Hansa's house and put the binder on the living room table. I suggested that Hansa and her husband Suresh read it. The following day I asked. "Have you read anything?"

Suresh had read "Uprooted." His first comment was, "The custom of greeting elders is to touch their *feet*, not their *toes*." He added that he had not been able to come to Delhi to meet me, but after reading the chapter, he felt like he was there. He also commented about Babu-ji and suggested I write a separate chapter on him. He described how difficult it had been for Babu-ji to tell the parents of the woman Madhu was engaged to that their daughter's engagement was off because

Sharing the Draft of My Memoir with Indian Family and Friends

he was marrying an American.[53] Suresh also wanted me to write more about Mandi customs.

Hansa didn't read anything the first day, but the second day she read late into the night. She voiced a strong reaction about the restaurant scene where we had our first breakfast in Delhi. She insisted. "There was no way that the waiter used the same cloth to wipe the crumbs on the table and then the dishes. It was an upscale restaurant in Connaught Place, and this never happened."

I argued with her, saying. "I saw it, and this was common in restaurants."

Hansa did agree with other incidents that she read about.

After eighteen days in Mandi, we left for Delhi to catch our flight to Boston. We stayed with our friend Ashwani Kapur and his wife, Seema. They had a modern home in Gurgaon, a suburb of Delhi near the airport. After a morning shopping trip on our last day in India, we returned to the Kapurs' house, and I showed them my memoir. Ashwani looked at the chapter titles and said, "I'll start reading it after lunch."

While he read the memoir, Madhu and I took naps. When we got up, we joined the Kapurs for afternoon tea. Ashwani immediately talked about the memoir. He said. "Your project is a great idea. You have captured your experiences in a vibrant manner." He suggested that I write more about women's education, widowhood, Chamba customs, the plight of the forests in Himachal Pradesh, and Mandi culture. He recommended that I read the *The Mandi State Gazetteer*, which was written by an English man.[54]

He also spoke highly of my father-in-law, Babu-ji. He thought that Babu-ji didn't extend his government service job because of a controversy with the chief minister. He added. "If Babu-ji hadn't retired at age fifty-five, he probably would have become the first Himachal High Court Judge and possibly a Supreme Court Justice."

Another comment Ashwani made was that I should compare how things were in the 1960s and 1970s with what they are like now. This was also suggested by members of my Nashua, New Hampshire, RISE (Rivier Institute for Senior Education) writing class.

---

[53] After the broken engagement, the woman was married to a Mandi man who was related to my brother-in-law Suresh. I met her on occasions and our conversations were limited.

[54] Emerson, G.C.L Howell, H.L. Wright Indus Publishing, 1996 - Mandi (India: District) - 205 pages.

Ashwani's wife, Seema, had read a few chapters. She commented. "I am amazed at all you went through at such a young age."

I was pleasantly pleased with the interest friends and family took in the draft of my memoir. Their comments were helpful. I immediately planned to do more writing using their suggestions. It was just one of so many ways that they all helped me throughout the years.

Epilogue

In 2011, I retired from my teaching job in Lowell. This gave me more time for family, friends, senior education classes, writing, bridge, doctor appointments, and household chores. Now that Madhu was also retired and living in Nashua, I was glad to have him join me in many of the activities. His favorite was being with our grandchildren.

We missed India. Family, friends, and Indian culture drew us back for yearly visits to Madhu's homeland, and we were so thankful to have the opportunity to go there. At the same time, our family in the United States and the American way of life were incentives to continue living here. It was a special bonus to have our daughters, their husbands, and our grandchildren living nearby.

On June 11, 2015 my life changed in a new direction. Madhu lost his battle with mouth cancer and passed away in his sleep at our Nashua home. Family and friends quickly joined me to share in my grief and support me. Madhu was cremated according to Hindu rites. A simple Hindu ceremony was performed at the Manchester crematorium

Elma and Madhu at their 50th wedding anniversary

chapel. In the near future I plan to visit India to take Madhu's ashes there so they can be sprinkled in the Ganges River.

After fifty-three years of marriage, there is a huge empty spot in my life. However with all that has happened, I know that my Indian and American friends and family are there to help me in my life.

Sometimes, I think of the well-meaning comments of my friends in India: *"Aap Hindustanti hain."* ("You are an Indian.") Yet, I am an American, too. As I look back over all these years, I feel very grateful for this special journey that has allowed me to be both. Whether my plane lands in Delhi or Boston, I always feel like I've come home.

Appendices

appendix a

Bucket in a Well

Uprooted! A blind date at Duke University, marriage to Madhu, and a move to India in 1962 were life-changing and challenging experiences. My first year living in northern India, I was a curious, uncertain, fearful bucket being lowered into a deep, dark stone well for collecting fresh drinking water. As soon as I arrived in Delhi, six months pregnant, I was immersed into Indian society. My in-laws, other relatives, and acquaintances were all Indian. I had no contact with Americans.

As the inquisitive, unsure bucket kept getting lower and lower, it got darker and darker in the narrow stone well. Living in India, I kept meeting different people, tasting strange food, observing new customs, and hearing an unfamiliar language. There was a continual push to become a part of this new world. It was tough for me.

Eventually the frightened bucket reached the surface of the water at the bottom of the well, floated for a while, and then started sinking to collect water. At this point I was drowning in Indian customs—a loss of freedom, and the pressure to conform to Indian ways. The long wait for Madhu to secure his promised job in the forest department seemed to go on forever. I desperately wanted to return to America and wished Madhu had accepted the forestry job that he had been offered before leaving the United States.

Gradually life began to change as the hopeful bucket filled with fresh, clear water started to rise. I began to come to grips with my new life and feel comfortable with Indian customs. I started to understand Hindi and was able to speak with friends and family. I liked the smell of roasting spices, fresh ginger, garlic, and onions. Now that I wasn't pregnant, curries and lentils tasted delicious.

As the smiling bucket reached the top of the well, there was light. After a few years in India, things began to make sense. I started to understand what was going on around me, and there was a comfort level with many situations that had initially felt so strange. I began to get used to the long waits, some of my mother-in-law's ideas about child-rearing, and differences in managing an Indian home.

Finally, the safe bucket filled with clean, cool, fresh drinking water was pulled out of the well. Everything was clearly visible in the daylight after Madhu got his forestry job. We moved from living with family to our own home in a remote valley town located along a snow-fed river stocked with trout. The new freedom to raise our son, Raju, as I wanted, was a breath of fresh air.

The bucket in the dark well filled with clear water had risen. Darkness changed to light as I adjusted to my new life in India.

Appendix b

A Letter from Madhu

Recently our daughter Rita found a letter written by her father to her while she was working at the Wyndham Hotel in Atlanta, Georgia. At that time Madhu was still living in India. I had returned to the U.S. and was working in Lowell, Massachusetts. Our daughter Tara was working in Hadley, Massachusetts at Smith College.

When Rita showed me her Dad's letter, I was amazed to see how well Madhu had expressed himself. Usually he was a man of a few words, but in this letter, he wrote a lot about our relationship, being exposed to two cultures, and Rita's move to the US.

Here is an excerpt from Madhu's letter written from Shimla where he was the Managing Director of the Himachal Pradesh Forest Corporation.

October 29, 1991

Dear Rita,

………

Exposure to two cultures has its plus points—in fact there are more plus points than there are negative points. It depends on your own mental outlook. Marrying Mummy I feel I have done a good thing and if given the choice again—I honestly feel that I would still marry her. Something about which I am very proud and feel lucky to have her as my wife. As we grow old, I think, both of us are getting more attached to each other. Someday I hope you find a life partner that you will love and your love grows deeper as the case has been with us.

A Letter from Madhu

Whatever you may do, please remember that you have lived in India for a long time—in fact your informative years were spent here and you should try to keep the good traditions that you have inherited here. It hardly matters where you live so long you maintain your contacts with your relations and friends here. I hope you will be visiting Shimla frequently in future even if you decide to settle in USA. It is no doubt a hard life here and if I were you, I would live in USA but would visit every year my relations in India. Whether you can afford to do so, only future can tell. But you will have a house here and in Mandi to come and stay.

......

Love,
Daddy

I am so pleased that Rita kept this letter and showed it to me. It is a very special memory of Madhu

Appendix C

Before and Now: India in the 1960s and India in the 21st Century

As this memoir details, in January of 1962 I married a graduate student, and six months later I left my homeland, the United States, to start a new life in my husband's homeland of India. During my twenty-five years of residing in India and during subsequent visits, I experienced drastic changes from the 1960s to the twenty-first century. Here are a few of the ones that stand out most to me.

Airports

Before (1960s)—On arrival at the Delhi airport, the first shock I felt was when the hot air blew into my face as I climbed down the open-air staircase to the asphalt tarmac. We walked to an ancient-looking building, passed through custom and immigration formalities, and went into the arrival section. None of the rooms had air conditioning, and the ceiling fans did little to alleviate the heat. As far as I recall, there were no shops or restaurants in the Delhi International Airport. In the 1960s, there were no televisions in the airport or anywhere else. It felt like I was in a small town, domestic airport rather than an international one.

Now (21st Century)—Fifty years later Madhu and I visited India after our move back to the United States. The Delhi International Airport was totally remodeled. I was amazed by the variety of modern, air-conditioned shops. They ranged from stores with Indian clothing to the latest technology devices. Smart phones, iPads, laptops, and other modern devices were displayed in the windows and aisles of the stores. As we walked to the baggage area to pick up our luggage, we passed Wi-Fi stations that hooked up to the internet for a small fee. On one wall, I saw a large-screen Samsung television broadcasting the news, with smiley faces for the good news and frowns for the bad.

Bathrooms

Before—My first shower in India occurred in a family friend's home in an affluent section of Delhi. At one end of the bathroom was a flush toilet but no toilet paper. At the opposite end was a faucet on the wall, three feet from the ground, and a small stool. There was no tub or shower. To wash up, it was necessary to fill a plastic bucket with cold water (hot water needed to be heated in the kitchen). Then you used a small cup to take water from the bucket. Once you were wet, you could soap up and then use more water to rinse off. It was important to use only one bucket of water, since there was often a shortage of water.

The bathrooms at my sister-in-law's house at Shimla were more basic. In one bathroom, there were four wooden commodes with metal buckets, which were cleaned by sweepers living nearby. These people belonged to the *Shudras*, the fourth class of people in Hindu society. Again, there was no toilet paper. The separate shower room with a cold cement floor had no running hot water. Water was heated in the kitchen and brought to the room in a metal bucket.

Now—The bathroom scene is very different. During my visit to India in March of 2012, one of the best bathrooms I encountered was at the home of one of Madhu's high school friends. The bathroom floor had grayish-white speckled tiles. There was a bathtub with a flowered, green shower curtain that matched the pale-green tub. The flush toilet and sink were the same pale green color. A hot water heater supplied running hot water for bathing. All kinds of soap, crème, and shampoo bottles were lined up on a shelf. I noticed a few American brand names. There was even toilet paper next to the flush toilet.

Kitchens

Before—While staying at Shimla in 1962, the kitchen consisted of two small, dimly lit rooms. Both had gray cement floors and smoke-stained, wooden walls. The first room had a small wooden table with shelves above it. There were brass cooking pans lined upside down on the shelves. The second room had a single-burner, brass kerosene stove on the floor, and a charcoal fireplace for cooking along the back wall. The fireplace was made from molded clay and had four holes for charcoal.

Now—Modern Indian kitchens look very different. Wood fireplaces, charcoal burners, and kerosene stoves are replaced with gas and electric burners. Gas stoves have one to four burners, which are hooked up to a red gas cylinder. These stoves are lit with matches or a clicker starter. Kitchens have running water with an electric boiler for hot water. Also, there are water purifiers for drinking water. Some kitchens have marble and granite countertops. Flooring usually consists of fancy tiles or marble chips set in cement. Pots and pans are aluminum, metal, and nonstick. Updated pressure cookers are often made in India, and some are exported to the U.S. Microwaves are standard fare in modern kitchens.

Role of Women
Before—In the 1960s there were few career women. Many married women stayed home to take care of their children, husbands, and in-laws. There were a few exceptions. Women doctors, called lady doctors, usually continued in their profession after marriage and after they had children. There was a big need for lady doctors since women didn't like going to male doctors. Some teachers and nurses continued in their professions after marriage, but many left their jobs to care for immediate and extended family. This often happened with their first pregnancy. Most of my friends were stay-at-home moms. Two of Madhu's sisters had children and did not work outside their homes. His third sister had no children and was a government social worker.

Most marriages were arranged by the parents. First preference was to find a match within the caste. In Mandi, parents also tried for a match within the town. Dowry was customary. Mandi dowries included gifts of clothes for extended family members. Many pieces of gold jewelry were given to the bride. Immediate family also received a gold necklace, earrings, or a ring. In some areas of India, when women didn't bring enough dowry to their in-laws, they suffered. In extreme cases, they were murdered by being doused in kerosene and then burned. (I don't think this occurred in Mandi, which had a kinder dowry system with less demands.) Divorce was uncommon, even if men were straying. When a woman became a widow, life was difficult. Diet, dress, and lifestyle changed drastically. Widows didn't eat meat, garlic, or onions. It was thought that these food items increased the sexual drive. They wore plain clothes, often a white *dupatta*, three-foot scarf worn around the neck or over the head, with their plain *salwar kameez*, baggy pants and shirt, or they wore a simple sari.

Now—In the twenty-first century, women work in many different fields and usually continue in their jobs after they marry and have children. This has become an economic necessity. Women are doctors, nurses, dentists, teachers, administrators, clerical workers, engineers, computer programmers, social workers, police officers, and other workers. Many women drive cars, scooters, and motorcycles. They have much more say in family decisions and at work. Some families are starting to refuse dowries from the women's families. In Mandi, there are practically no dowry demands. Divorces occur when marriages can't be saved. Widows have less restrictions.

Foreign Exchange

Before—It was extremely difficult to get foreign exchange in the 1950s and 60s. When Madhu came to the U.S. in 1956, his travel agent, Thomas Cook, was able to secure foreign exchange from the Federal Reserve Bank of India to pay for his ticket and an additional $7 for his travel expenses. There were places in Delhi where he could have gotten dollars by paying an outrageous price to black marketers, who dealt in illegal exchanges. In 1966, I wanted to travel to the U.S. for my first time home and tried to buy a plane ticket, which needed to be paid for in foreign exchange. After several trips to the Reserve Bank of India and phone calls asking my Dad to send proof that he would support me during my visit, an official finally gave the foreign exchange for my ticket.

Now—Foreign exchange was liberalized after 1991. Now it is much easier to exchange rupees for dollars legally and at the market rate. Credit cards and ATM cards from Indian banks can be used in the U.S. and other countries. When using the cards abroad, the money is deducted from an Indian bank account, which is funded with rupees. Some Indian banks issue cashier checks in dollars that have been paid for in rupees. Banks encourage Indians living abroad to make deposits in dollars and other foreign currency.

Schools and Colleges

Before—There were private elementary and secondary schools in the towns and big cities. As an American citizen living in India I couldn't work in a government job, but I was able to obtain a visa to work in a private school. There were some private colleges but not as many as the private schools. Private professional graduate school colleges were rare in relation to the need. The government colleges for doctors, engineers, lawyers, and business people admitted only a small percentage of students taking the entrance exams. More were needed.

Now—There are many private professional colleges, which are known as donation colleges. If students don't get admission in the state engineering, business, or medical schools, they can apply to donation colleges. If accepted, they will pay much higher fees than state schools. Often these donation colleges cost ten to twenty times as much.

Jobs

Before—When I first came to live in India in the 1960s, the favored jobs were with the government. Engineers, doctors, teachers, nurses, clerical workers, and others preferred to work for the government, which had first-rate salaries and excellent job security. Private-sector jobs were limited and often didn't have as good benefits.

Now—Now there are many private hospitals, schools, technology firms, engineering companies, software firms, call centers, and other businesses that have jobs with good pay and good benefits. Many of these jobs are with Indian companies, which have outsourcing contracts with foreign companies. Often people prefer these higher-paying jobs with good avenues for promotion.

Foreigners

Before—In the 1960s there were few foreigners living and working in India. Most of them were in big cities. I rarely met any foreigners my first years in India, and none resided where I lived. The Stokes family from Pennsylvania did settle in Himachal and brought the American Delicious variety of apples to the upper hills of Himachal. They lived in parts of Himachal where I never lived. In the 1980s, I met two Americans who stayed in Dalhousie. They were two hours from our Chamba home, so I only visited them occasionally.

Now—In the twenty-first century there are many foreigners coming to India to work in technology companies, outsourcing businesses, and other firms. Some come for short stays to check on work being done in the companies, and others stay for years. Bangalore has many firms that are owned and run by Americans.

Phones

Before—Landline phones were hard to get in the 1960s. Usually they were not available in small towns and villages. In cities, it took a minimum of two to four years to get service. It often required knowing the right person or offering a bribe. Cell phones were nonexistent.

Now—Today, cell phones are everywhere. They outnumber landlines. Big cities and small villages have cell phone towers. Villagers and city folk walk around talking on their cell phones. Upper, middle, and lower classes own cell phones. On my last visit to India I was surprised to see so many drivers with phones. Even more surprising was watching the domestic help in my own home using their cell phones. I could never have imagined this when I first moved to India.

Cars

Before—In the 1960s, Ambassador cars, Willy's jeeps, Tata-Mercedes-Benz trucks, Fiat cars, and diesel buses plied the roads. They were manufactured in India. On rare occasions, I saw a foreign-made car. Many of the cars were owned by the government and used by officers. Some well-off individuals owned cars, usually only one. Most were driven by hired drivers. Women drivers were rare. In the 1980s I was the first woman driver to get a license in Chamba district where I lived.

Now—In the twenty-first century, many makes of cars ply the roads. Indian and foreign car companies have factories in India. Maruti Suzuki is the number-one-selling car. Its popularity is boosted by dealerships and service networks in small towns and rural areas. Other popular cars manufactured and sold in India are the Ford Ecosport, Honda City, Hyundai Grand, Tata Nano, and Volkswagen Jetta. Middle-and upper-class families often own more than one car. Many drive their own cars, and women are among the drivers.

Politics

Before—The political system in the 1960s was mainly a one-party system with the Congress Party ruling. Congress Prime Minister Jawaharlal Nehru ruled from 1947 until his death in 1964. Two years later his daughter Indira Gandhi, a member of the Congress Party, was elected Prime Minister.

Middle—Between the 1970s and the turn of the century, second parties began to gain power. Many of these parties were offshoots of Janata parties. By the 1990s the Bharatiya Janata Party (BJP) became a second powerful party, winning elections in Uttar Pradesh and other states. Their leader, Atal Bihari Vajpayee, was Prime Minister for three nonconsecutive terms of thirteen days, thirteen months, and five years. His third term was from 1999 to 2004. His oratorical, organizational, and leadership skills enabled the BJP to accomplish much during his term. Vajpayee is credited with opening the Indian economy to foreign investors and building roads to connect villages to their district headquarters.

Now—In 2015, there are many political parties with lots of competition from non–Congress Party members. Vajpayee greatly aided these changes. He was followed by Man Mohan Singh, a Congress Party Prime Minister. Still there were many active non–Congress Party members in the state and national political arena. In May 2014 the BJP had a landslide victory. Narendra Modi became the BJP Prime Minister, and there was no coalition government.

Which Is Better: The 1960s or the 21st Century?

As shown here, some of the positives in the twenty-first century are improved kitchens, modern bathrooms, more car owners, better private-sector jobs, advanced technology, increased private graduate schools, a two-party political system, availability of foreign exchange, and more rights for women.

However, these positives come with negatives. Profitable, private-sector jobs throughout the country result in job seekers leaving their home states and moving to places far from extended family. More women in the workforce mean children see less of their mothers. When men and women take jobs far from their hometowns, they lose the support of in-laws and parents. Often elders don't want to leave their hometowns, or there isn't space for them in city apartments. This means elders can't help with grandchildren and don't have adult children to care for them. Of course, they have their phones and Skype to keep in touch, but it's not the same as living together.

Even huge improvements in the transportation system also come with disadvantages. Increased cars on the roads create major traffic jams, and finding parking spaces can be a nightmare.

I like the twenty-first-century improvement in homes, private-sector enterprises, technology, and transportation. However, I miss the 1960s, particularly the intimacy of extended family members living in close proximity. Family spread across the country and abroad is a negative in the twenty-first century.

Glossary

A
Aa jao   come in
Aap   you
Accha   good, very well, understand
Admi   man
Akshar   a letter of the alphabet
Aloo   potato
Aloo tikki   fried potato cutlet with spices
Ama-ji   respected mother
Angithi   a small metal box with burning charcoal
Arya Samaj   a branch of Hindu religion

B
Bacha   baby
Bada Mama-ji   respected elder uncle
Badi Mata-ji   respected grandmother
Bahar   outside or out
Bahut   many, very, enough
Beedhi   Indian hand-rolled cigarette
Bhajan   prayer
Bhatura   Indian roti made from yeast or starter
Bhawan   guest house
Bhookh   hungry
Bindi   red dot worn on a woman's forehead which historically had spiritual meaning, but now it is more of a fashion statement
Burfi   Indian sweet made from thickened milk

C
Chai   tea
Chaukidar   caretaker

Choti Mami   younger aunt
Chutney   a sweet-and-sour spicy sauce

D

Dadi   paternal grandmother
Dahi bhalla   a doughnut-looking lentil preparation soaked in yogurt
Devta   Hindu god
Dhaba   tea stall
Dhoti   long piece of white muslin cloth wrapped around a person's waist and legs
Doodh   milk
Dosa   fermented crepe stuffed with potatoes
Dukan   shop (noun)
Dunghard   sleeping arrangement where bedding is laid out on the floor
Dupatta   long muffler-like scarf worn by women with a salwar kameez
Dupher   daytime

E

Ek   one

G

Galt   mistake
Ghal   timber transported by being floated in a river
Ghee   clarified butter; butter cooked until there is very little moisture content
Gorkha   person from Nepal
Gujjar   buffalo herdsmen, Muslims

H

Hai/hain   are
Hamara/hamari   our

J

Jhord   cooked buttermilk with turmeric and other spices

K

Kachori   roti stuffed with lentils
Kadoo ka khatta   pumpkin cooked in a sweet and sour sauce
Kajal   black eyeliner
Kameez   long shirt
Kanchi mordh   a sharp turn on a road shaped like open scissors
Kapre/kapray   cloth or clothes
Khanna   food

Glossary

Kheer   rice pudding
Kshatriya/khatriya   second highest social class, traditionally military or ruling class
Kurta pyjama   a long shirt with a high collar worn over Indian pajamas

L
Larka   boy
Lotha   small metal cup

M
Mama   uncle
Mandiali   a dialect of Hindi spoken by the people of Mandi
Matar panir   peas and Indian cheese
Mela   village/local fair
Memsahib   polite form of Mrs.
Mirch   hot peppers
Momos   dumplings stuffed with meat (a Tibetan dish)

N
Namaste   a greeting
Namaste-ji   a more respectful greeting

P
Pahari   mountain person
Pahari topi   a hat worn by Himachal mountain people
Pakoras   deep fried vegetables in a batter of chickpea flour seasoned with hot peppers, turmeric, salt, coriander, and cumin
Palki   stretcher-like arrangement with a fancy chair and canopy for carrying gods and goddesses
Pandit   a scholarly religious leader comparable to a minister or priest
Parantha   a roti that is layered with oil before cooking on a griddle
Peon   office attendant
Poori   Indian fried bread
Pyar   love

R
Roya   cried
Rupees   Indian currency

S
Sahib   a polite form of Mister
Salwar kameez   baggy pants fitted at the ankles and worn under a long shirt

Samajh gai   understand
Sari   a drape anywhere from five to nine yards (4.57 metres to 8.23 metres) in length and two to four feet (60 cm to 1.20 m) in breadth that is wrapped around the waist, with one end draped over the shoulder. A short, fitted blouse that bares the midriff is worn with it
Satyagraha   passive resistance (advocated by Mahatma Gandhi)
Sham   evening
Subha   morning
Subzi mandi   vegetable market
Subzi wala   shopkeeper
Sundar   beautiful
Suntra   orange (fruit)

T
Tambola   a game like bingo
Tawa   griddle
Tehsildar   assistant magistrate
Tiffan   stacked, metal containers for carrying food

U
Upama   vegetables cooked in cream of wheat (a South Indian dish)

Made in the USA
Middletown, DE
14 April 2016